Date Due

OCT 4			
DEC 8			

The Slow Learner
and Music

A HANDBOOK FOR TEACHERS

J. P. B. DOBBS

LONDON
OXFORD UNIVERSITY PRESS
NEW YORK   TORONTO
1966

Oxford University Press, Ely House, London W.1

GLASGOW NEW YORK TORONTO MELBOURNE WELLINGTON
CAPE TOWN SALISBURY IBADAN NAIROBI LUSAKA ADDIS ABABA
BOMBAY CALCUTTA MADRAS KARACHI LAHORE DACCA
KUALA LUMPUR HONG KONG

Printed in Great Britain by
The Bowering Press Plymouth

Preface

THIS book is one of the outcomes of a process of experiment and exploration made possible by a generous grant from the Carnegie United Kingdom Trust. This enabled us to bring together, in the first place at a week-end Conference at Wye College, a group of people with a variety of skills and experience in the teaching of music; they had one thing in common, a profound interest and concern in the education of handicapped children. What emerged from the conjunction of these interests was an awareness of the need for further and more methodical exploration of this field, for the collection of information about materials and methods and for the provision of courses of training for teachers of handicapped children. With the backing of the Carnegie Trust we were enabled to translate our enthusiasm into practise and plan a pioneer short course. This was held at Gilbert Murray Hall, Leicester, in July 1964.

This was a memorable experience, no less for the planners and staff than for the members, for indeed we were all learners in this field. Undoubtedly we benefited from the 'Hawthorne effect', the enhancement of enthusiasm and achievement which results from association with experiment and pioneering. But there was more in it than this. For we were, while exploring the use of media and methods, searching for the basic principles involved in learning new skills, and this was done by subjecting ourselves to experiences and situations similar to those in which our pupils learn.

Naturally we also learned a good deal about the

planning and conduct of courses of this kind and hope to embody the fruits of this in future courses. Meanwhile, in the chapters which follow, Mr Jack Dobbs has delineated the territory and summarized the fruits of our joint experience in so far as these can be overtly described. It should serve to inform and encourage workers in this difficult but rewarding field of education.

J. W. Tibble.

Contents

Foreword

IT is estimated that about a tenth of the children in this country are backward in their educational attainments. They range from children whose work is just below the normally expected standard to those who are on the verge of 'ineducability.' No single word is adequate to describe so heterogeneous a group, and they are met under different names in different schools. In its recent pamphlet, *Slow Learners at School**, the Department of Education and Science has defined its own use of the most common terms:

'It is proposed to use the term "backward" or "slow-learning" for children of any degree of ability who are unable to do work commonly done by children of their age. The word "dull" will be used for those who have limited mental potential and the word "retarded" for children whose poor educational achievements appear to result from factors other than limited general ability. In the context of this pamphlet "retardation" is used to convey a general notion of underfunctioning without specifying whether such a condition is necessarily remediable or implying that an assessment of general ability is closely related to the extent and rate of progress possible in a specific field.'

These terms are used with a similar meaning in the chapters that follow.

This short extract shows the diversity of the children included under the comprehensive umbrella of the term 'slow learners'. Their common bond is a *need*—the

* *Slow Learners at School*, Education Pamphlet No. 46 (H.M.S.O., 1964).

need for a special education that is designed to help each of them develop his or her own mental potential to its fullest extent. A small proportion of them* will be educated in a day or residential special school. A much larger number will attend the normal schools of our Local Education Authorities whose duty it is to provide for them the special educational treatment they require. Since the passing of the Education Act of 1944, how far has the section dealing with the slow learners been implemented, and what more can be done by all who teach in Primary, Secondary Modern, Comprehensive, and Special Schools to ensure that they receive an education designed to meet their individual basic needs, whatever their age, ability, and aptitude?

This book attempts to answer the second part of this question in relation to one of the activities of the curriculum—music. I believe that music has an important —indeed essential—contribution to make to the education of the slow learners, and I hope that this brief introduction to a vast and largely unexplored subject will encourage more teachers to experiment imaginatively with music in their special groups, classes, and schools.

Since our children vary so considerably in the causes and extent of their backwardness, it is not always possible to specify the exact age-group for which any given activity is most appropriate. The suggestions will also have to be considered in the context of the particular type of school (e.g. day or residential), and the organization (e.g. streamed or unstreamed classes) within the school. The way in which the singing material and listening music has been arranged in the Appendices

* In January 1963 there were 379 special schools in England and Wales catering for nearly 38,000 educationally sub-normal pupils.

may help teachers to select what seems most suitable for their own children.

The chapters that follow summarize work that has been done with teachers in various parts of the country over a long period, and in particular with a group of teachers who attended a week's course at the Gilbert Murray Hall, Leicester, in July 1964. This course, which was organized by the Standing Conference for Amateur Music with the financial help of the Carnegie United Kingdom Trust, was the first national residential course concerned with music in the education of the slow learners to be held in this country. Its staff* met on several occasions during the previous year to plan the project, and the ideas they shared then are incorporated in this book, together with the methods by which these were translated into practice during the course itself.

Whilst acknowledging my debt to all the tutors mentioned below, I must accept sole responsibility for omissions and for inadequacies of expression and presentation. I am especially grateful to Professor J. W. Tibble for his Preface, to Miss V. Bruce for her contribution on Movement and Dance, and to Mr. M. Lane for his assistance in compiling the Appendices.

* Professor J. W. Tibble (Director of the course), P. F. C. Bailey, Grace Barrons Richardson, B. Reaks, R. L. Bishop, M. E. V. Lane, Dr S. Northcote, J. K. Owens, E. M. Raymond, R. Roberts, Angela Tyrrell, J. D. Watkins, Sophia Williams, Mabel Wilson.

1

The Children—and the Value of Music to them

SLOW learners vary greatly in ability and behaviour, and until we can recognize some of the features that distinguish them from each other as well as from other children, we shall not be able to devise for them the special education in music they need. Moreover, although they may be described as belonging to certain groups (the dull, retarded, etc.), and obviously we must understand the difference between these groups, we must always remember that our real concern is with the individual *within* the group—with the physical, mental, emotional, and social growth of each unique child. Such growth has no one rate or prescribed pattern.

(a) Probably the most easily recognizable group consists of children whose limited potential affects all they try to do. Their handicap is innate, and it is unusual to find any activity for which they have a special ability. But there are exceptions, and occasionally a special ability for one of the creative arts is discovered amongst them.

The ablest members of this group will be capable of absorbing a limited amount of knowledge and of developing certain skills. Their general rate of learning will be slower than that of their fellows in a comparable age-group, and the quality and range of their learning, as well as its rate, will be affected. Nevertheless, when they are placed in a favourable environment and given the appropriate stimuli at the right time, many of them may surprise us by the amount they can achieve, and we must always beware of demanding too little from them.

It is very important that we should make quite certain that what appears to be a permanent condition in the children of this group is not just the temporary result of a sensory defect which could be alleviated by the appropriate medical treatment.

(b) A second group of children in need of special education are not limited in innate intelligence, but have become retarded because of absence from school through illness, or because of a number of changes of school. They have missed important steps or processes required for the understanding of a subject, and whilst other children have continued to make progress they have stood still or slipped back. The gap between their own achievement and that normally expected from their age-group widens, and worry and frustration colour their approach to all their work. Other children who are not limited in their general intelligence have specific learning difficulties which slow down their rate of progress, particularly in those subjects which receive the greatest attention in schools, and in which the stages of attainment are most easily measured.

(c) The true quality of intelligence of another large group has failed to find expression because of some emotional blockage. Any environment which hinders the healthy development of a child's emotional life is also likely to hinder his intellectual growth. Some children may not know the security that can be found in a family which gives its members care and love. They may come from broken homes, or from homes where tension exists between the parents: others have homes which appear happy and stable on the surface, but in which they are stifled by over-protection, or made anxious by the intellectual and social standards expected from them. To the mental handicap of some children is added a physical incapacity. This prevents them from joining freely in normal leisure pursuits and tends to make them withdrawn and introverted. The feelings of bewilderment, disappointment, and resentment which many of them share absorbs so much of their creative energy that little of it is left for their learning and living.

(d) At the junior stage we must watch particularly for slow developers who appear to be limited in intelligence only because they fail to reach the standards set for their age-group at the normally expected time. With help and understanding they will begin to blossom when they are ready, and then continue to make rapid progress in both their learning and their general maturity.

At some stage the children in all these groups will need the special education of which the 1944 Education Act speaks, but from the brief indications given it will be clear that the form this education takes will vary considerably. It will vary for each of the main groups, and it will vary according to the needs of each child within the groups.

As has already been suggested, one of the most important needs of all children is the need for security. Whatever their home background may be, they can still find this security in many Infant Schools. Here they mix with their friends in an environment which has some of the qualities of a stable family. The emphasis is on creativity and co-operation, and the children are too young to worry about degrees of educational attainment unless they are forced to do so by over-anxious parents. But when they move to on the Junior Department some of them are not yet ready to face the more formal teaching and the competitive element which is still sometimes found there, and which is likely to remain while the value placed on children depends upon their academic potential. Our slow learners must be judged according to their own potential, not according to their success as compared with that of their more able friends. Success within one's own limitations may be accounted failure outside them.

Many of the attitudes to learning which cause such serious problems in the Secondary School first appear at this early stage. Unfortunately, the present size of classes in Primary Schools and the dearth of teachers with appropriate training and experience make it impossible for some of the slow learners to receive the individual help which they require if later difficulties are to be prevented. To the anxiety communicated by their parents is now added their own anxiety to satisfy parental expectations, and despair saps their confidence as they begin to realize that they just cannot make the grade which has been arbitrarily fixed for them.

As well as wanting to please their parents, children want to please their friends and be accepted by them. This is not always easy for the slow learner who for various reasons, including, perhaps, a physical incapacity, may not be able to join fully in the games and play through which his fellows develop socially and emotionally. Children can be cruel to each other, and make life unpleasant for one of their number whose physical appearance or lack of cleanliness becomes a subject for comment amongst them. They can also get very impatient with the slow child who cannot keep up with them in their pursuits. How can we expect a child who is aware of failure in his work and of rejection by some of his schoolmates to show any real interest in the activities we have designed for him?

When a runner finds himself getting left farther and farther behind in a race, it takes a lot of courage and determination for him to keep going at all: much easier to drop out and slink unnoticed away from the track. To feelings of failure and inferiority is added apathy. Why bother?'

From this situation there are two quite common avenues of escape for our children. They can withdraw into their own world of day-dreams, or they can express their frustrations and feelings of inadequacy through mischievous and aggressive behaviour. And so in the special class we may find two groups with quite different characteristics. In one the children are lethargic and lacking in initiative, with no sparkle in their eyes and no apparent awareness of their immediate environment. Because they rarely create any disciplinary problems it is easy to forget their existence altogether. In the other group the children are easily distracted, fidgety and noisy, drawing attention to themselves by every means at their disposal. Both groups are likely to play truant and stay away from school frequently with illnesses of a psychosomatic or imaginary nature.

All the problems which are present in embryo in the Junior Department will be found in a more concentrated form in the Secondary School, if the new entrants are treated as rejects who have failed to make the grade. On arrival at their new school some of them may give the impression of being lazy; but their apparent laziness may be due less to an antipathy to work than to unhappy attitudes towards it, or to an inability to exert the necessary physical effort, because of a low standard of all-round fitness. Frequently, too, they are tired through insufficient sleep, for such reasons as emotional disturbances, overcrowded homes, late watching of television, or early rising for odd jobs to supplement the family income. They may be inadequately fed, in that their diet—although sufficient in quantity—may lack nutritional value. It is true, of course, that these factors can be found in varying degrees in the homes of many children, but they are rather more common in the homes of the children we are considering.

As the backwardness of the slow learners is often accompanied by a degree of social and emotional immaturity, they do not always react to a given situation in the manner that is expected from their age-group. Their behaviour depends more upon impulse than considered judgement, and they can easily be led into undesirable and anti-social activities which may, at some stage, take them to court.

They need to be skilfully directed and guided, but they also need to experience the exhilaration of independence and the satisfaction that comes from accepting responsibility. Complete dependence on other people is enervating to the personality, and the child who is always on the receiving end is denied one of the greatest pleasures of life. Growth in confidence and self-respect begin to appear as soon as the child is given the opportunity to make an independent contribution, however small, to the group. Paradoxically, it is often in homes that appear least satisfactory that he gets this opportunity, for the parents from some of the apparently 'better' homes become so over-protective that their children never get a chance to develop their own initiative. Certainly adults should help and guide, but but they should also know when to leave well alone.

Parents and teachers have to balance very carefully the two basic needs—security and independence. They must devise activities which will enable both to be satisfied—activities that are sufficiently demanding to stretch the child to the limit of his capacity, and yet not so impossibly difficult that he is discouraged because he cannot perform them successfully. Like all of us, he wants occasionally to bathe in the warmth of success and to know the assurance of adequacy. Like us, too, he is better able to bear failure in one direction if he has already experienced success in another.

Having considered some of the emotional states and behaviour patterns to be found in our children, let us look briefly at their physical condition. About this it is equally impossible to generalize, although it is agreed that there is a greater incidence of minor physical disabilities and physical retardation in children with a low level of intelligence than in normal children. Some of them show an all-round physical growth equal to that of other children, but have a greater difficulty in co-ordinating their movements; others develop unevenly in certain aspects; and others although physically well-developed are emotionally immature, and so not in complete control of their physical urges. Yet others, in contrast, are underdeveloped physically but fairly mature emotionally and socially.

Stammering, indistinct articulation, and general speech retardation are also found more frequently amongst them. These may not always be due to physical defects in the speech organs or brain: they may be the

B

result of an unfortunate background, or a by-product of some deep-set emotional condition which they, in turn, help to aggravate. Visual and aural defects are also common, but these, too, may often be traced to a source which is not entirely physical.

And then there are the regular troubles which are familiar to all workers with these children—running ears and earache, catarrhal and asthmatic conditions, adenoids and sore throats, and common occurrences like headaches which may be psychosomatic in nature. Finally there are the severe physical handicaps (e.g. cerebral palsy and blindness) which some of them suffer in addition to their mental handicap. All these conditions, slight and severe, imaginary and real, must be taken into account by teachers who are probing to find the reason for their pupils' backwardness and for the various attitudes they adopt to learning and the school environment.

These, then, are our children and some of their basic needs. Where does music fit into this picture? Has it any special contribution to make to their general education, and how far can they be involved in the musical activities of the school?

Having seen something of their emotional needs, we must recognize that only an education which can help to satisfy these has any real significance for them. This is the great strength of music, for it powerfully influences the emotional life of all human beings. It can produce in us emotional responses (gay music makes us happy), and it can express for us the emotions we are already experiencing (when we are happy we want to sing or whistle gay tunes). By awakening in us positive emotions it can stimulate us to more purposeful living, and by acting as a channel for the release of our emotions, both positive and negative, it can contribute to the re-creation of our personalities.

Its impact on us at this emotional level does not depend upon the quality of our intelligence. Of course the fullest understanding of music demands an intellectual apprehension, as any attempt to understand much contemporary composition will soon prove. Nor is an artistic vocal or instrumental performance possible without the use of a high degree of intelligence, together with other faculties like patience, concentration, and perseverance which are not possessed by the slow learners to any great extent. But we are not expecting to produce creative musical geniuses or accomplished performers from children with limited mental capacities. That would be unrealistic. Our primary aim is not to train them as musicians so much as to educate them as people through the impact music makes upon them. We hope that the pleasure they get out of their music, the sensitivity it develops in them and the discipline they learn from participating in its activities will help them to grow into happier, more mature personalities, ready to play a worthwhile part in the life of the community to which they belong. We hope, too, that some of them will come to appreciate more deeply the music to which they have been introduced, and will want to continue making it when they have left us.

Through music they are able to join in activities with their companions without the fear of failure and inferiority, for it has so many facets that they can all enjoy the satisfaction of achievement in some of them. A carefully selected musical activity need not demand more of a child than he can give, but it does create situations in which he can be stretched to his limit—

and he enjoys being stretched if he is really absorbed in what he is doing. We must avoid any competitive element in the activity we choose, and design it so that the child who joins in after a long absence from school or a change of school does not feel left out or discouraged. Fortunately, the logical series of steps and dovetailed processes required for the progressive understanding of some subjects are not essential in many of the simpler musical activities. Much of the responsibility for the success of these will depend on our own skill as teachers and 'encouragers' to draw out from the child and nurture the elements of music which are already lying dormant within him.

By providing him with opportunities for achievement through the accomplishment of work well done within the limits of his ability we shall help to build up his confidence. This means, of course, that the work must be carefully graded so that continuing progress is ensured for each individual at every step. Weeks spent patiently building up this confidence can be turned to no account by the choice of inappropriate or impossible tasks. The experienced teacher will be quick to recognize this moment by the reactions of the children, which will vary from complete withdrawal to stubbornness and defiance.

On the success achieved in one activity and the confidence engendered by it, other successes, perhaps in the basic subjects, may be built. And if the child's backwardness is due not to inherent dullness but to an emotional blockage, the initial success in music—with all the favourable attitudes to learning created—may give him just the impetus he requires to sweep away the blockage and reveal the true measure of his intelligence and maturity.

In music the satisfaction of achievement can come to a child both as an individual and as the member of a group, for many of his activities will be organized in a group context. It is very valuable for our children to learn in this way, co-operating with each other and sharing their experiences, so long as we remember that each child also has his own individual rate and pattern of development. The integration of individuals into a social group through choral singing, singing-games, movement, and performance in instrumental ensembles is especially needed by children who tend to be lonely or unco-operative, and who, in compensation, sometimes gang up with their fellows in less desirable pursuits. Carefully selected group activities give each child a degree of responsibility for the success of the whole, but do not lay on him more responsibility than he can bear.

Music can relax the bodies and minds of children who are over-tense, whether they are taking part in musical activities or just listening as they lie quietly on the floor. The effect of such quiet listening is impossible to assess, but there have been occasions when it has brought to the surface of a child's mind repressed memories which have been hindering his healthy growth. Music can arouse the apathetic pupil from his state of lethargy, making him more active and lengthening the span of his attention. It is sometimes the only thing that will encourage the very withdrawn child to leave his shell of reserve and communicate with the world around him. By its evocative powers it can extend his horizons and stimulate his imagination. Through instrumental work and other physical activities like singing-games it can be used to help discipline, control, and co-ordinate the movements of our children which are often more jerky and clumsy than those of normal children.

Above all, it can give to every child real pleasure, not only in school, but during leisure hours at home and on holiday. To those of us who have many ways of getting our pleasure this may sound hardly worth mentioning: but for children whose home background is not always as happy as might be desired, whose activities are necessarily limited, and whose friendships may not bring them complete fulfilment, such pleasure in music-making with its accompanying sense of well-being and exhilaration can do much to compensate for their lack of other opportunities. Not only do they get pleasure themselves, but they can give it to other people—to their schoolmates and families and to various organizations in their neighbourhood, to those who love music and to those who, if judged on their musical aptitude and knowledge would, perhaps, prove more backward than our own children. For this reason, if for no other, music can claim a central place in their education. The capacity for giving is one of the most precious qualities of any human being, and without it no personality can become truly mature.

2

Music in the Life of the School

BOTH singers and instrumentalists agree that they make greater progress when they are able to practise regularly every day, if only for a short time, than when they have to fit all their practice into the same amount of time divided between only two or three periods. Regularity and continuity of practice are as necessary for children as for professional performers—and particularly for young children who are making their first acquaintance with musical activities. If we really want music to mean something vital to them, the 'music lesson' time-tabled once or twice a week must be replaced by more frequent periods of music-making unrestricted by a rigid time allowance.

If this is true for normal children, how much more true is it for the slow learners whose powers of attention and span of concentration are not so great. A daily spell of activity, however short, is likely to ensure greater progress than the same amount of time divided between two fixed lessons several days apart. Whatever the general pattern we decide upon, there must always be room within it for flexibility of time allowance according to the interest created by the activity and the needs of the children on any particular occasion. Some activities may have to continue longer than we anticipated because of the children's complete absorption in them: others may have to be curtailed because external circumstances—perhaps just the weather—make the group so restless that all their concentration disappears. It may not be appropriate to have music at the same time every day, and the placing of the music-making within the framework of the school's other activities—some stimulating, others relaxing—will tax the teacher's ingenuity to the full. This time for music will not be labelled *Singing, Theory, Appreciation,* for it cannot be pigeonholed into such neat compartments as that suggests. Appreciation is a quality that must permeate all our work from the moment we sing or play our first note, and theory gains significance only in the context of such practice. Each period must contain as much variety as possible within the time available so that there is something in it to attract the interest of each of the children, and some activity designed to cater for every individual ability. Each period, too, should be reasonably self-contained, so that children who are frequently absent do not feel left out because of the lessons they have missed.

But music is not just a segment of knowledge to be studied: it is an activity that can add colour and excitement to a variety of occasions. The birthday of a child in the class calls for a musical celebration, so does a happy local or national event, and each of the seasons of the year can be marked by its appropriate carols and dances. What about songs for the various stages of the day? 'Good morning' songs, grace before the midday meal, and 'good-bye' songs in the afternoon; a musical welcome to the new entrants, and a musical farewell to pupils when they move on to the next Department? For the older pupils there will be community singing on their tramps, at the School Camp and in the Youth Club. For all there will be music at the daily act of worship. Some ways in which music can be related to other time-table subjects are described in Chapter Seven. This music-making will be additional to that of the recognized periods, and being integrated into the general life of the school and the everyday events of the children, will help to break down the artificial barriers that have been built up between 'school' and 'other' music—'ours' and 'theirs'.

Nor should we forget the power of music to revive the children when they are getting lethargic, and to calm them down when they are over-excited. If they are growing tired of what they are doing and their interest and concentration are beginning to flag, the spontaneous introduction of a bright song may help to enliven them and freshen them for their next activity. Sometimes, on the other hand, they come into the classroom from the playground or a physical activity so stimulated that they need relaxing and calming before they can settle down to their next session of work. At such a time a carefully chosen record or a solo played on a quiet melodic instrument may help considerably.

The argument often advanced as examinations or selection tests approach, that music takes essential time away from the more 'basic' subjects, has been magnificently refuted in the Primary Music Schools of Hungary. These schools, pioneered by Zoltán Kodály, differ from the country's other primary schools only in the greater proportion of time they allot to music. But it has been proved that their pupils do just as well in their general subjects during examinations as any other children—often better. The disciplined training required for their musical performances and the pleasure they get from them make them more ready and willing to give themselves with greater zest to their other time-table subjects.

What has been said above can generally be worked out in terms of practice within the organization of the normal Infant and Junior Schools as easily as in the Special School, because it is assumed that there the teacher responsible for music with the younger children will also be in charge of all their other class work. It is more difficult to break down the divisions between subjects in a Secondary School where a specialist music teacher is responsible for the music of all the children—including those who receive special educational treatment. His time-table will have to be worked out to the last minute, even if theirs is not.

If what has been said about the basic need of the slow learner for security is valid, it follows that the person who is with him for most of the time, who shares his interests and general activities, in whom he can confide, and whose attitude is dependable and predictable is also the person who should be responsible for his music. He can relate it to the child's other activities and every-day living much more satisfactorily than a specialist who sees the group only a few times a week. This is certainly so in the early stages of education: I think it is true for a longer period with our children whose need for security is sometimes even more urgent during their first years in a Secondary School where specialization is, at present, the usual practice.

Some teachers will claim that this is impossible because they cannot teach music. If they really are incapable of it, or if they are likely to convey a positive dislike of the art to their pupils it would certainly be better for them to leave it severely alone. But the number of such teachers is smaller than is generally believed, and some of the best practical work done, even in Grammar Schools, is the result of the musical enthusiasm of a nonpecialist who is able to convey his own whole-hearted enthusiasm to his pupils. Too often one finds that the Scoutmaster who, on a Saturday evening has led a successful camp-fire which included songs and rounds from all over the world is hesitant about teaching music to his class on a Monday morning because 'school music is different'—and he isn't a pianist.

But why should school music be so different and the piano be held in such awe? With young children especially, a large upright piano can be more of a hindrance than a help, and with every age-group it tends to make the lesson too teacher-centred. If instruments are required for accompaniment, there is a wide variety of simple ones available. They can be played by both the teacher and the children, and as they are portable they can be used in the classroom, in the dining-hall, in the playground, or in any other place where the children gather together. More information about these instruments is given in Chapter Four.

The musical activities described in this book have been selected with the non-specialist in mind. Almost all of them can be undertaken by any teacher responsible for special education who is musically sensitive, enthusiastic, and ready to spend some time and thought on the preparation of his material. Much of his learning can be done *with* the children, and the joint progress made will be a source of satisfaction to teacher and taught alike.

Just as our music-making will not be limited to what goes on in a 'lesson', so neither will it be confined within the walls of the school. The school must take its music out and share it with the local community, and in its turn the local community must bring its music-making into the school where it can be related to the children's regular activities. There should be more combined music-making by the children and their parents, and we must be alive to any sound or television programmes that can forge a link between the school and the home. By these means we hope that music will begin to play a more relevant part in the children's lives and that parents will see that the effectiveness of our teaching in school can be considerably affected—for good or ill—by their own attitude in the home. It may also help to remove the misconception that school is the place where children 'prepare for life', with its implied corollary that it is only in the world outside its walls that they begin to live.

3

Singing Together

UNLESS the slow learner suffers from a physical defect of his vocal organs he is likely to have a singing voice which is potentially as pleasant as that of other children, but he may be hesitant about using it freely. If he is withdrawn he may shrink from expressing himself vocally at all: if his early efforts have been silenced he may have lost confidence, and if he comes from a home in which there is no singing he will have had no pattern to copy. But when he can be persuaded to join in he usually gets great pleasure from his singing, and the activity itself can be beneficial to his general health as well as his emotional development. We must do everything possible to encourage him to participate by creating attractive musical situations in which he will want to be involved.

Children will sing freely only when they have confidence. They have this unselfconscious confidence when they are very young, and we must be careful to do nothing that would undermine it for them. Our attitude must be one of quiet and constant encouragement. We must praise any promising feature, however small, and avoid showing the disappointment we may be feeling when the tone produced is not as beautiful as we would like. In these first stages it is important that the children should express themselves confidently, even with 'mistakes': frequent interruptions and niggling criticisms quickly discourage them and make them feel that this is just another activity in which they are going to be failures. This does not mean that we ourselves should rest satisfied with their performance. They will never achieve their potential if our own standards are too low, and we should always be looking for ways in which we can improve the quality of their singing. Children who have grown accustomed to shouting about their homes must gradually be made to realize that this is not the sort of sound we want, and children who have been forcibly silenced at home must have their confidence restored so that they will not be afraid to participate. They are imitators, and when we are listening to the sounds they are producing we might remember that these are, in some measure, a reflection of those we are patterning to them.

Young children imitate melodies which are sung to them more readily and accurately than those which are played on the piano, and so it is important for us to pattern the songs we are teaching with our own singing voice. Such patterning can be done by more teachers than is generally believed. It involves three basic requirements—the knowledge of a variety of nursery rhymes and simple songs appropriate to the age-group being taught, a confident use of the natural singing voice, and the ability to make the songs come alive.

For the acquisition of a varied repertoire of songs it is not essential to be able to read music, although an understanding of tonic sol-fa or staff notation will obviously give us a greater independence and open for us the whole treasure store of musical literature. There are other ways of learning songs—e.g. from the singing groups of such organizations as Scouts and Guides and the Youth Hostels Association. The Folk-Song Clubs are another rich source of material, and perhaps some time we shall have in this country a movement like the *A Coeur Joie* of France, which teaches its members a common corpus of songs which they can share together and then pass on to other people they meet. Within the school we may be able to learn from other members of staff or a local music specialist. If we cannot learn in this way from other people—and such oral transmission has positive advantages—we can, perhaps, garner our material from one of the BBC's programmes—e.g. 'Listen with Mother' for the very young, and 'Singing Together' for older children. A list of records on which suitable songs are presented in an imaginative manner is given in Appendix C (ii).

In order to pattern songs we do not need the highly-trained voice of a professional soloist. The voices of some professional performers sound so strangely unfamiliar and remote to our children that they make no impact on them at all. They prefer a less sophisticated voice that is warm and expressive, that speaks directly to them, that sings the words so that they can understand them, and that conveys the mood and dramatic import of the song so vividly that they want to join in. With the expressive voice must be associated an expressive face, and where appropriate, expressive gestures. 'Expression' is not an extra that is 'put into' a song when the words and tune have already been learnt. Slow learners need more than words to help them to understand what the song is about, and in front of her group the singer must become an actress forgetting her natural reserve and self-consciousness as she identifies herself with the song she is singing.

The teacher cannot communicate directly with the children in the ways suggested unless she can be seen by the whole class. This is not possible if she is seated behind an upright piano, and much of the force of her personality will inevitably be lost if she sits with her back to a part of the class for any length of time. It is more possible if she is fortunate enough to have a mini- or baby-grand piano for her use; but even these instruments can form a barrier between herself and her singers, and so prevent her personality from making its full impact. The best seating arrangement for our children, senior as well as junior, is often in the shape of a fat horse-shoe, with the teacher forming the focal point at the open end, where she can both see and be clearly seen by all. This direct contact between the children and the teacher's personality is of paramount importance.

If the teacher feels embarrassed without an instrument to support her voice—and she will be more aware of its absence than will her children—she can, perhaps, learn to play a guitar. The guitar is a very versatile instrument. Its quiet sounds will not distract from her singing voice, but it can also produce considerable volume, and it is capable of many and varied dramatic effects, percussive as well as melodic and harmonic, should these be required. For the accompaniment of most of the folk-songs we teach only the common chords of I (doh), IV (fah), and V (soh) will be required. With a guitar the teacher can sit in her focal position, or she can carry it with her as she moves amongst the class, encouraging the shy, enlivening the apathetic, and making the restless aware of her presence.

At least two other instruments are useful for providing a simple accompaniment—the auto-harp and the chordal dulcimer. To play a chord on the auto-harp, the teacher has only to press down the bar labelled with the figure and letter of the chord she requires and draw her finger-nail or a metal plectrum across the strings. The instrument is obtainable in several sizes (3-, 6-, 9-, and 12-bars) and the number of chords and keys available vary according to the size.

The chordal dulcimer is even simpler in construction, and is also made in several sizes. In some schools it could be made in the craft shop. Across the sound board of the smallest one there are three sets of tunable strings which produce the most frequently used chords: I, IV, and V. All the teacher has to do here is to pluck the set of strings of the chord she requires or strike it with a small wooden striker which has felt on one side of its head to provide a different tone colour. The sounds produced by both these instruments are attractive to children and blend well with their voices. The volume is not sufficient to provide an adequate accompaniment for a large class, but in special education we can expect to be dealing with small groups—and the amount of sound is quite big enough to support the teacher's own voice. Neither the auto-harp or the chordal dulcimer is as easily portable as the guitar. Various ways in which the children can create their own accompaniments with pitch and rhythm percussion instruments are discussed in Chapter Four.

Although some of the dangers of being tied to a piano have been mentioned, and although the absence of a piano need not imply the absence of music-making, there are nevertheless times when teachers who are competent pianists will want to use it for accompaniment purposes. Some songs have piano accompaniments without which they are incomplete, and improvised accompaniments to the different verses of other songs can add colour, atmosphere and dramatic effects.

Even so, we must still make sure that a close relationship has been established between ourselves and the children before we embark on any pianistic flights of fancy.

The teacher can, of course, only present the song convincingly if she has so absorbed it into her system that it has become part of herself, and she can sing it without a book. Imagine the effect on an audience of a 'pop' group singing their songs from the books they held in their hands, and looking, perhaps, as if it was the first time they had seen them. The book will be kept to be referred to only when necessary. Teachers may be pleasantly surprised at the sense of freedom this gives them.

Although the teacher's facial expression is so important, it is sometimes helpful for the children to listen to her singing with their eyes closed so that they can concentrate all their attention on the sound. This is basic aural training, and such training in listening is especially valuable for our children. It is helpful, too, if the melodies of songs to be learnt can be heard on a variety of instruments (e.g. the recorder or violin) at times which are not thought of as singing periods. Some of these melodies will make very suitable introductory music at the daily act of worship, and if we cannot play them ourselves, perhaps we can persuade some friends to put performances on tape for us.

Whatever the age-group we are teaching, it is important to get the children singing as soon as possible: they want to see quick results in all they do. Both the words and the melodies of the songs will have to be taught by rote to all the younger children and to most of the older ones, too, because of their limited verbal reading ability. But we can involve them in the singing straight away if we choose songs that divide naturally into sections that can be sung by the teacher, followed by short jingles, repeated phrases, or refrains that can be quickly learnt by the children. From some children we can expect only one or two words in each verse, e.g. 'Noah' in 'Who built the Ark?' and 'Cuckoo' in the Czech carol, 'The Birds'. And sometimes the word will be spoken, not sung. For older pupils sea shanties are valuable. They divide naturally into the main narrative of the shanty-man and the short rhythmic refrains to which the sailors did their pulling, pushing, or hauling. Negro spirituals also often have a main section with a number of short repeated phrases, and the same division can be found in other more recent American songs like 'Li'l Liza Jane'. If the teacher sings the verses in a way that catches the imagination of the children they will begin to join in quite spontaneously according to their interest and ability, and most of them will finally be able to sing the whole song, verses as well as refrains.

The lines of the verses should be fairly short and the number of verses in a narrative song or ballad cut to the minimum which is necessary to make sense of the story. The words should be simple, direct, repetitive, and within the grasp of the children's imaginative understanding, clear in meaning and with no complicated tongue-twisters. We must give careful thought to this matter of words. The singing of well-chosen songs can help the child who has specific speech defects, improve articulation generally and enlarge and enrich the vocabulary of all. For children who are severely retarded in speech the *Articulation and Activity Songs* and *Mouth Imagination Songs* of John A. Harvey (publisher W. Paxton) will prove helpful. Teachers whose primary responsibility is remedial speech education and not music agree that the melodies and rhythms of songs can help children in their articulation of the sounds of the words, and that better results are often achieved by the use of words sung rather than words spoken. The improvement is likely to be more marked in the vowels: consonants cause more trouble. This is a field of activity in which the music teacher and the speech therapist can co-operate fruitfully.

The songs will make a greater impact when they are dramatized whenever appropriate. Such dramatization will come quite naturally through the teacher's use of her own voice, face, and gesture: but it is also good to involve the children as fully as possible. The whole class may take part in the acting, or a small group may be chosen to mime the story whilst the rest of the class sing. As well as bringing the song more vividly alive, miming will give the children an additional medium of expression. In the mime they can live out their fantasies and find a creative channel for their emotions. During it they can identify themselves with other characters, and live at a different and perhaps more exciting level. Their powers of observation will be increased and their imagination developed in sensitivity. It is sometimes in a wordless mime to music that the very withdrawn child spontaneously speaks for the first time. Gaining confidence from this initial step he gradually becomes more willing to speak freely before the class.

As a large proportion of the children's education reaches them through their eyes the use of visual aids will help them to memorize the sequence of events in their songs—pictures drawn on the blackboard, hanging up in chart form in front of the class, cut out of paper on their desks or changed rapidly on a flannelgraph.

The songs will need frequent repetition. Our children

enjoy the familiarity that comes from repetition, but the repetition of any activity for repetition's sake is value-less: it becomes purposeful only if the activity has made an initial impact on the children and encouraged them to want to participate in it. Although not refer-ring specifically to music the following extract from Ronald Morris's book *The Quality of Learning* (publisher Methuen) is pertinent here:

Much, indeed, would be gained if as teachers we should come to place less reliance on drill, repetition and the slow-building-up of blind habits and devote the energies saved in this way to discovering more precisely the exact nature of the intellectual difficulty that confronts a dull child and to devising learning situations that would help the dull learner to gain insights into his problems and to learn, as the bright child does, by the active organization of his own experience.

It is often said that our children have poor memories, but memory depends on attention and that, in turn, on interest. Perhaps the material we choose is so irrelevant to the interest of the child that he has no desire to remember it. It is noticeable that words are usually memorized more easily and accurately when they are wedded to an attractive tune. The child who finds it difficult to remember the order of sentences in the Lord's Prayer can often sing them with comparative ease, and it is surprising how long a child will remember a quite complicated cumulative song like 'The Tree on the Hill'.

From the musical point of view the songs should have a fairly limited pitch range and a strong, easily grasped rhythm. Those in ternary form (ABA, or AABA) or rondo form (ABACA) are obviously easier for the children to memorize than those which have a different musical phrase for every line of words and a different tune for every verse. Their delight when a familiar tune reappears is clearly seen on their faces. As many backward children are shallow breathers they have a comparatively small reservoir of breath to draw upon, and their breath control lacks steadiness. Both of these factors will determine the length of phrase we can ask them to sing. We must do all we can to enlarge their capacity and develop their control without making them breath conscious. Fifty years ago Stewart Macpherson stressed the importance of good breathing habits to the general health of children:

'The singing class has a very distinct value in the development of the child, for when it is conducted on the right lines, he has the chance of learning the art of correct breathing, a matter the importance of which is being increasingly recognized at the present day. In fact, many medical authorities consider that there are not a few ailments which may be checked, if not cured by its means.'*

And many years before that John Curwen, known to most of us for his work with Tonic Sol-fa, had written about the same subject:

'One use of singing is, however, seldom remembered—that is, that it promotes health. Indirectly it does this by giving a flow of spirits and chasing away weariness and despondency. But it does this also directly by the exercise which it gives to the lungs and to the vital organs. We cannot sing without an increased action of the lungs and this causes the heart and all the organs of digestion and nutrition to work with renewed vigour. The singer brings a greater quantity of air in contact with the blood, and hence the blood is better purified and vitalised. Healthy and highly

* *The Musical Education of the Child* (Joseph Williams, 1915).

oxygenated blood gives benefit to the brain, and thus the mind, as well as the body, shares the benefit of the exercise.' *

There are usually more monotone singers amongst our children than in normal classes after the lower junior stage. This is rarely due to a physical disability of the vocal mechanism, although there may be slow development of the muscles governing the vocal cords, and a weakness of muscular co-ordination. It is more likely to be the result of prolonged lazy listening, lack of perception, and an inability to understand what is required. Often the necessary remedial treatment has not been available at an early enough stage. Some of the children come from homes where there has been little singing for them to imitate, perhaps because of large families in a cramped space, a lack of interest on the part of their parents and incessant background noise from a record player. Being slower in their general development, they will take longer to learn from those around them—teachers and fellow pupils—than will the more able children from a similar environment.

We must involve them as fully as possible in all our musical activities, and during the singing class place them right in the middle of the children who can pitch their notes. Frequently they must be sung to directly by the teacher—and not only when the songs are being patterned to them. Occasionally we might sing to them what we would normally say, and encourage them to try to sing back their response. Simple question-and-answer songs can be attempted, with the teacher improvising a short question at a suitable pitch and asking the children to make up an answer to it.

It will help the 'growlers' to get the feeling of the rise

* *How to Read Music and Understand It* (J Curwen & Sons, 1881).

and fall of the pitch if they use movements with their hands and other parts of their bodies, and if we draw for them on the blackboard a picture of the shape the tune is making. Notes played to them on a xylophone or similar instrument hanging up (with the smallest and highest notes at the top) will enable them to see that 'high' is 'up' in the series of notes and 'low' is 'down'. Some normal infants take a little time to grasp this concept, and we must remember that our backward juniors are still at the infant stage in many aspects of learning. In this matter of pitch the piano gives no visual help since the 'high' and 'low' of its keyboard are both on the same horizontal level.

A careful choice of song melodies will help. Some melodies introduce quite difficult leaps at speed before the singer has had time to establish himself on the note which is going to act as the springboard for the leap. They may be suitable for children of the chronological age for which they are suggested, but not for the vocal abilities of our own pupils. One of the best ways of helping the growler is to give him a pitch percussion instrument like a chime bar and encourage him to sing with it as he plays. More detailed methods of training children to pitch notes can be found on pages 102–5 of the *Infant Book* in the *Oxford School Music Books* Series. In the early stages the imitation of wailing sirens, revving motor cycles, and other such noises may give children a better understanding of the rise and fall of pitch than any formal training.

Some of the difficulties we meet when teaching singing to our children, such as wandering attention, lazy listening, and breathiness are caused by the condition of the children's general health. Many slow learners have noticeably less vitality than their fellows. If this is organic in origin it will need medical attention, but it may be due to the conditions which were described in Chapter One, and which we may be able to help remedy. Real improvement in their singing will depend on a change in their manner of living (e.g. a reduction of their starch intake may lessen the frequent catarrhal complaints from which many of them suffer), and over this we do not have complete control. But, as has already been suggested, the very act of singing can be a tonic to them, and the more they enjoy it the richer will their personality become. This will be reflected in the more expressive quality of their tone and the greater vitality of their performance.

Their enjoyment will depend to a large extent on our choice of songs. Through these they can express their various moods and emotions, and they need as great a variety of them as of the moods they experience: songs which are gay and sad, serious and humorous, stimulating and soothing, songs for marching and dancing, songs suitable for school journeys, camps, and festivals. We shall probably find that we are concentrating on the bright, gay songs to 'cheer them up', and yet their own choice is often for slow, even melancholy ones. They must have songs through which they can express their sadness as well as their joy.

The children's own choice of songs and requests for repetitions give us an insight into their interests and hobbies and an indication of the subjects that particularly appeal to them. Another way of getting to know more about them while developing their imagination and creative abilities, is to ask them to make up their own words to some of the melodies they sing. A number of our folk-songs with very beautiful tunes have words which are either inappropriate or too difficult for our children. With the children's own words they will take an honoured place in the school's repertoire. If the words are based on a central event or story, some of these songs can be linked together to make a simple ballad opera, a project which will combine many activities and departments at both the junior and senior levels. Perhaps we can learn something about the singing of melodies *without* words from the French group 'Les Swingle Singers'—and we should remember that most boys, and many girls, enjoy whistling.

One of our biggest problems is to find songs that are sufficiently simple in their words, melody and rhythm for the slow learners to sing, and yet are suitable in subject and mood for their chronological age-group. A slow learner of fourteen doesn't really enjoy songs which express the sentiments of a child four years his junior— however educationally sound the words and music may be. Songs which are written down to what is considered to be a child's level must be avoided like the plague. In Appendix B there are listed some of the songs which have proved successful with children at various stages.

Unfortunately some of the books which contain the most suitable songs for backward seniors are labelled 'Junior'. This, of course, does not matter if they are seen only by the teacher, but there are at least two reasons why they should also be used by the pupils from time to time. One is that any regular link between ear and eye will help towards the reading of notation, and the following of music notation may develop eye movements helpful to ordinary reading. Our children are not incapable of gaining some understanding of notation, and some of them will surprise us by their fluency in reading rhythms. We, too, can learn with them. The other reason for using books is that the children enjoy handling them: they know other classes and streams use them, and they don't want to be treated differently. It would help if their books were so illustrated that the story of the song was made reasonably clear to the non-reader, and if the printed notes were sufficiently large for the children to be able to run their fingers under them when following the melody.

Singing games involve the younger children in a group activity that combines singing with movement. In them the withdrawn child is encouraged to make contact with other children, and sometimes does so when all other methods have failed. They provide opportunities both for a certain amount of free movement and for movements which are closely directed by the patterns of the game. Children who lack confidence can work within the context of guidance, and the more adventurous can use their own initiative. The words and movements may have to be simplified to suit the understanding and physical abilities of the group using them. Any movement or action which adds meaning to a song is valuable, so long as it isn't superimposed in the rigid, unimaginative way that was characteristic of some of the 'action' songs taught to previous generations.

A collection of songs which teachers with very backward young children will find especially useful is *Children's Play-songs** by Clive Robbins and Paul Nordoff. This collection, as its title indicates, combines singing and children's play. A number of the songs contain questions and answers between individuals and the group, and by means of them all a considerable amount of basic teaching can be done on the children's own names, the days of the week, colours, speeds and counting.

* Theodore Presser Company, Bryn Mawr, Pennsylvania, USA. UK agent: Alfred A. Kalmus.

The majority of our songs will, of necessity, be in unison and even in these we shall have some difficulty in getting a satisfactory blend of voices: our children are individualists. It is much better for them to sing unison songs imaginatively and with comparative ease than to have their confidence shaken by attempting part-singing before they are ready for it. Some of them may never be ready for it. Nevertheless it has been tried and proved successful in the senior classes of some schools, and it has been found that the sense of independence gained from this achievement can be carried over into other activities of the school's curriculum.

Some training for part-singing is, of course, done in any song which involves individual characters with all the voices joining together in the chorus—e.g. 'The Mermaid'. Taking the part of a character presupposes the ability to sustain a solo, to time one's entry, and to provide appropriate vocal contrasts to the other characters. It is interesting to discover how many children volunteer for the solo parts.

At some suitable stage, and only the teacher will know when that is reached, rounds can be introduced. These must be short enough to be memorized quickly and have words which are meaningful and relevant to the children's experience and environment. The melody should be learnt as thoroughly as possible as a unison song with rhythmic and harmonic support from the piano or guitar if necessary, before any attempt is made to divide the singers into parts. After it has been learnt in this way, it should be left for a day or so to give it time to sink in, before it is brought out again to be sung in parts. The children should then take the first part with the teacher entering as the second voice, and only when this has been successfully accomplished should the opposite order of entries be attempted. Let there be as much variety of dynamics within the melody as possible, and the same sort of imaginative interpretation that one would expect from a unison song. There are three possible ways of ending a round—each part can finish separately, all can end on a chord together, and each part can sustain the last note of its own part until all have finished. In the first and last cases each part sings the complete melody an agreed number of times; in the second, each part will have a different amount to sing —e.g. in a 3-part round where part 1 sings the whole melody three times, part 2 will sing it $2\frac{2}{3}$ times and part 3 will sing it $2\frac{1}{3}$ times. Don't be discouraged if the conducting proves a bit difficult at first. For the sake of variety, instruments may be substituted for one or more parts, or for just a phrase within a part—e.g. the 'ding, ding, dong' at the end of 'Frère Jacques' sounds very effective on chime bars.

Some simple canons are possible when a piano can help rhythmically to keep the two parts together or when two groups can be joined and two teachers made available to lead the separate parts.

Teachers have noticed that many of the backward boys lose their treble voices rather earlier than boys in other streams—and are proud of the bass sounds they produce. For these boys participation in simple SAB singing is sometimes possible if the arrangements are chosen carefully. These will include a preponderance of unison singing with a division into parts only occasionally—perhaps just at the soh-doh cadences for the bass-baritones, with a simple step-wise part for the altos to complete the harmony. Although the senior children in the special class usually prefer to stay in their own groups for most of their singing, it can give them a great boost to join in a 3-part choir made up of children from the other streams where they can be carried along in their parts by the more able singers.

This chapter has concentrated almost exclusively on singing, but it is hoped that this will not be taken to imply that singing is a separate and isolated activity. It should be related as closely as possible to listening, instrumental work, and all the other activities that are discussed in the following chapters.

4

Playing Instruments

NOT all children enjoy singing equally, and we should introduce our groups to instrumental activities as alternative—and additional—means of expression and communication as early as possible in their school life. From these they will benefit in a number of ways. The playing of instruments involves a co-ordination of mind and muscle, of the aural, tactile, and usually the visual faculties, and the effect of this training in co-ordination will extend beyond instrumental performance. The mental alertness it develops can also be carried over into other activities, and many teachers have noticed how much more lively their children are after an instrumental session. When a child becomes really absorbed in his playing he is happy to continue it for quite a long time, and as he does so his span of concentration is gradually extended. The control he gains over his instrument gives him a feeling of achievement, and this, together with his growing sense of confidence, will be further increased by any successful public performance in which he takes part. Although his audience for this 'public' performance may be only his class or the rest of the school before whom he plays as a member of the instrumental ensemble at Morning Assembly, the acceptance of responsibility it involves enables him to take an important step forward in independence. For both shy and aggressive children the social training and discipline which is implicit in any ensemble work is of great value. The child's desire to play an instrument provides him with an incentive for learning to read staff notation, and the excitement of performance gives him the determination to persevere.

In his early days at school his approach to instrumental work will be empirical, and will involve many of the experiments with sound that are suggested in the next chapter. The instruments used for this purpose may be home-made from simple materials or commercially produced. In either case, they should be appropriate for the stage of physical and mental growth reached by the children who are to play them, they should be instruments that the children enjoy playing, and the sounds they produce should be beautiful in quality. Some home-made instruments can produce very beautiful sounds, and some commercial instruments very ugly ones—but the opposite may also be true. Those of us who are just beginning to teach music might be wise to take a more experienced friend with us when we are making our purchases.

The material we need for making simple instruments will often be provided for us by our own children. Already inveterate collectors, they can usually find plenty of wooden boxes, small tins, rubber bands, various types of bells, coconut and walnut shells, pebbles, beads, cotton reels, and perhaps old inner tubes. The methods by which this miscellaneous assortment of bits and pieces can be transformed into shakers, rattles, clappers, drums, xylophones, chimes, one-stringed banjos, etc., are clearly described in a small booklet by Kathleen Blocksidge called *Making musical apparatus and instruments for use in nursery and infant schools* (published U.L.P.). Pictures of all the instruments are given, together with detailed measurements of the materials.

required. At first we may have to make these ourselves, but usually it is not long before some of the children will want to join in and help us, or be responsible for a complete instrument themselves. If the making of an instrument will in any way stimulate the child's interest in the playing of it, encourage him to treat it carefully, and make use of any creative ability he may have with his hands, he should certainly be given the opportunity to do as much of the work as he can. When completed, the instruments may be used for free experimentation, and for accompanying the children's own songs and the music we play to them on the piano or gramophone.

As an alternative, or in addition to these home-made instruments, there are the more orthodox rhythmic percussion instruments which can be purchased—tambours, drums, tambourines, castanets, rhythm sticks, wood blocks, Indian bells, and cymbals. The type of instrument must be chosen to suit the child using it, e.g. cymbals would not be given to the youngest: so also must its size. There is no reason why percussion playing should be limited to infants (every symphony orchestra has its percussion department), but if the instruments are used by seniors (e.g. as an aid to listening), they must be of an appropriate size. They should be of the finest quality both to handle and to listen to, and maintained in a state of good repair. We must firmly reject the offer of instruments which have already been discarded by other classes. Children whose powers of discrimination are most limited need the best instruments obtainable to help them in their efforts. Unfortunately, one still finds some schools in which the children with least ability are taught by the least experienced teachers, and given the least attractive and valuable equipment to use.

D

Let us think about the ways in which we can intro-duce the instruments to the youngest children, and the suggestions made can then, perhaps, be adapted to meet the needs of the older age-groups. During the period of experimentation we shall introduce the instruments into as many of the children's activities as possible—into their games, their poetry and dramatics, and the stories we tell them, to provide imitative or evocative sounds, and to create atmosphere. In their nursery rhymes the characters can be represented by appropriate instru-ments—e.g. in 'Jack and Jill', Jack can be played by the drum and Jill by the triangle: Jack and Jill go up the hill together; in the second line the drum will play phrase one and the triangle phrase two. Gradually the instruments will take on distinctive personalities with clearly recognizable tones of voice, and this will help the children when they begin to work out simple 'orchestrations' for themselves. The association of instru-ment and character in nursery rhymes also encourages the children to listen carefully and to remember the words of their rhymes. Unless the drummer is able to remember where Jack comes into the rhyme he will not be able to play his instrument in the correct place. Other ways of using the instruments are suggested in the next chapter, on listening.

At some stage we shall want the children to form a little band: but not the sort of uniformed band which is sometimes drilled for exhibition before parents and V.I.P.s on special occasions. This often involves too much regimentation, concentrated practice on one in-strument only, and the unvarying repetition of a printed score. There is no place in such a band for the withdrawn child. In the early days we are aiming at awakening the children's imagination to the quality and timbre of sounds, so that they will later be able to suggest to us what instruments will be most effective as accompaniments to the phrases, climaxes, and other structural features of the music to which they are listening. This communal working out of the orchestration—which need not be written down in score form, and which will leave opportunities for improvisation—will stimulate the children's creative abilities as well as train their powers of discrimination and give them practice in the playing of a variety of instruments.

As soon as the children have had an opportunity to get to know the feel and sound of their instruments, we shall begin to concentrate on their experience of the pulse, rhythmic patterns, and dynamics of the music to which they listen. This we shall do through their work in movement as well as through their percussion playing.

When they first pick up their instruments to perform as a group with the music being played on the piano or gramophone it is likely that neither pulse nor pattern will figure very prominently in their playing: there will probably be just an explosive din, with the children enjoying themselves greatly. But if our piano playing is sufficiently rhythmic they will soon become aware of, and caught up in the recurring beat which they will begin to tap out on their respective instruments. This will by no means be unanimous, but gradually they will discover that they are making similar hand and arm movements at the same time—they are playing together. This usually gives them a great deal of pleasure, and creates a strong feeling of unity which is increased as the players get drawn together into their instrumental groups—triangles, tambourines, drums, etc. The enjoyment and excitement of playing must precede any elaborate organizations of their positions.

Until we are happy that the feeling for pulse is firmly established we shall let all the instruments play together throughout the rhyme or song. Soon, however, we shall want to cut down the volume of percussive sound and arrange for some contrast of instrumental colour. There are several ways in which we can start doing this. In a four-phrase rhyme three instruments can each play one phrase, with all of them combining for the last phrase, making that the climax of the performance. e.g.

Half a pound of two-penny rice,	(*Rhythm sticks*)
Half a pound of treacle;	(*Tambourines*)
That's the way the money goes,	(*Drums—one stick*)
Pop! goes the weasel.	(*All three instruments*)

We can use question-and-answer rhymes, with different instruments representing the people asking the question and the same instrument answering them:

Pussy-cat, Pussy-cat, where have you been?	(*Drums*)
I've been to London to look at the Queen;	(*Triangle*)
Pussy-cat, Pussy-cat, what did you there?	(*Tambour*)
I frightened a little mouse under the chair.	(*Triangle*)

In this rhyme the triangle has been used to represent the cat. Some children find it difficult to control the triangle, and they may have to be given another instrument which contrasts with the drum and tambour. A little later we can emphasize the form of the tunes we use—ABA, ABACA, etc.—by the choice of our instruments. We shall, of course, do what we can to encourage variety of volume and tone colour within the phrases, but we must not expect too much subtlety of expression from our children in these early stages.

Usually they find it fairly easy to feel a steady pulse and maintain it on their instruments. Some of them have more difficulty playing rhythmic patterns, and we must watch carefully to discover whether this is caused by an undeveloped rhythmic sense, faulty perception, or a lack of muscular control. The instruments we have given them may not be suitable in size, and we may be they demanding quicker and smaller movements than are capable of managing.

We shall start with simple rhythmic patterns, identified, where ever possible with familiar words. A nursery rhyme in which the words and musical rhythm fit together well is 'Polly, put the kettle on' (first verse).

Pol-ly, put the ket-tle on,

Pol-ly, put the ket-tle on,

Pol-ly, put the ket-tle on; we'll all have tea.

The words and rhythmic pattern of the first two phrases are identical, and each of the verbal syllables has a note to it. The last line is an extension of this pattern, and should not be too difficult for some of the children to grasp. They can certainly join in the last three notes '*all have tea*'. The most frequently recurring unit is the rhythm of the name *Polly*. If the children are able to play *Polly* as they say it, they will soon be able to manage the whole rhyme. To provide practice in this type of rhythmic patterning we might devise exercises based on the children's own names, first spoken and then transferred to other instruments:

e.g. **Timothy Hughes**: played by the owner of that name, and then taken up by the other instruments:

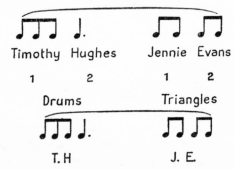

Rhythm sticks   Tambourines   Drums   All

We might then attempt to join two names together:

Timothy Hughes   Jennie Evans

1   2   1   2

Drums   Triangles

T. H   J. E.

Other names may be added. Later we shall substitute for the children's names the names of flowers, local places, football teams, favourite meals, 'pop' singers, or whatever else may be of particular interest to the group of children with whom we are dealing. Let us encourage as much improvised rhythmic conversation between groups in the class as possible. What may prove more difficult is the simultaneous playing of two different rhythms by the two halves of the class; but this becomes easier if the children keep in their mind a popular name associated with the rhythm they are playing—perhaps the class could be divided into supporters of two football teams. We may then have these rhythms being played together:

Wolverhampton Wanderers   Bristol City

1   -..   2.   -   1   -   2   -.

with an underlying pulse played on the drum by the teacher. For a change the children may put down their instruments and speak these rhythms through their hands and fingers, with the use of hand-claps, knee-slaps, and finger-snaps.

Some of them may not be able, in their percussion playing, to go beyond the stage of combining a pattern with a pulse: in other groups a third instrument may be played on the first beat of the bar by an instrumentalist who can count steadily. 'Polly, put the kettle on' may then be orchestrated in the following manner:

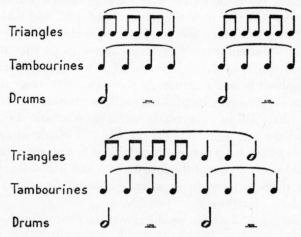

If the children are able to sing the melody with its words (the same line is repeated three times) the triangles need not play the pattern of the words. Instead, they could perhaps, repeat throughout the rhythm of the words—'*all have tea*':

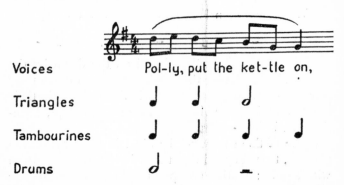

Voices	Pol-ly, put the	ket-tle on,	
Triangles	♩ ♩	♩	
Tambourines	♩ ♩	♩	♩
Drums	𝅗𝅥	▬	

Our score is now beginning to get congested, and we must see how we can let light into its texture (e.g. by letting the tambourines play on only the 1st and 3rd beats, counting mentally the 2nd and 4th), and where we can introduce special effects of orchestral colour. The children themselves may suggest to us that the final words of the first verse '*all have tea*' need more emphasis from the drums. At the appropriate stage the other percussion instruments will be introduced: the cymbals will be particularly useful for dramatic effects and the castanets for local colour. Our children may take a little longer than other children to get used to the hold and playing of the instruments, but it is valuable for them to have the experience of handling as many different instruments as possible.

So far we have not used any written charts. Some of

our children may never reach the stage of reading nota-tion—even rhythm notation. Others certainly will. For all, the experience of hearing and speaking—of absorb-ing and expressing—must precede the process of reading. Reading from a score, especially when it is written on the blackboard or on a chart in front of the class can aid concentration and weld the children together as a group. But it must be introduced at the right time, and care must be taken that it does not turn the playing into a mechanical exercise lacking joy, spontaneity, and vitality. Teachers who are inexperienced in the holding and playing of the instruments will find it valuable to attend one of the LEA or residential summer courses that are available. From these they will catch some of the excitement of performance that no reference book, however adequate, can convey.

In addition to the percussion instruments already mentioned, there is now a large variety of delightful pitch percussion instruments * on the market. They, too, need to be examined carefully before they are pur-chased, as their quality of tone and correctness of in-tonation varies considerably, even when they bear the same maker's name. With them we now have the chance of forming a small orchestra which will seem more grown-up to some of the children than a percussion band.

Some of the most useful pitch percussion instruments are the chime-bars. These may be bought separately, and their numbers increased as funds allow until we have the full range of two chromatic octaves available. Even if we can start with only one, this can be used by the children to add a pitch to the rhythm (e.g. Timothy Hughes) they have already clapped and tapped on

* Also called 'melodic percussion' and 'tuned percussion'.

their percussion instruments. The chime-bar has a lovely bell-like ring, and it can add incidental colour to stories, games, nursery rhymes, and songs—especially those which feature bells (e.g. 'Ding, dong, bell' and 'Frère Jacques'). With two notes (e.g. G and E) we have two pitches available for our rhythms, the opportunity for improvised conversations, and a cuckoo call —or two bells—to add to our songs and stories. The two bars G and D (taking G as 'doh') will provide a quiet accompaniment to many of our nursery rhymes. We could, for example, use them to accompany the first section of 'Polly, put the kettle on'— with or without the percussion orchestration already worked out:

With more chime-bars greater variety of accompaniment becomes possible:

or using the descending and ascending scale of G:

Here we may have to arrange the notes of the descending scale from left to right, and if we have enough bars available, it would help to duplicate the notes so that the children could continue in the same direction with their playing:

B A G F♯ E D E F♯ G A B

_____➔

With this larger number of chime-bars children can make up their own tunes. For this purpose, the pentatonic scale, d, r, m, s, l, d' and its arrangement s, l, d, r, m, s' are useful. Tunes created from these notes can start and finish where the child wishes, and whatever the order of notes the tunes will always sound attractive. Two children improvising tunes simultaneously will find that their two tunes fit together quite happily.

Some of our children will need fewer notes than this to start with, and we, ourselves, may be surprised to discover what interesting melodies can be made out of only three notes, e.g. 'Winter creeps' on the following page.

Win-ter creeps, Na-ture sleeps;
Fields are bare, Cold the air;

Birds are gone, Flowers are none.
Leaves are shed, All seems dead.

It is important that the children should have only the bars they are going to play in front of them. This makes it less possible for them to play a 'wrong' note: the choice left to them is in the order of notes or in missing the chime-bar altogether. For the same reason such other pitch percussion instruments as glockenspiels (diatonic and chromatic), xylophones and dulcimers should all have detachable metal or wooden notes, and the tubular bells tubes which can be removed from their frames, leaving only the notes the children need. The cheaper models of these instruments often have fixed notes, and it is not easy, even for adults, to select the required note from a complete series. The extra cost for a good instrument will be money well spent if it prevents 'mistakes' and so preserves confidence in these early stages of playing.*

In performance, the player must avoid stiffness of the wrist, so that the striker can rebound easily from the chime-bar or instrument slat: without this rebound, the vibrations will be damped, and the magic sound characteristic of the instrument and so appealing to children lost. Further details about the instruments and methods

* The Studio 49 instruments of Carl Orff are obtainable from Schott, 48 Great Marlborough Street, London W.1.

of playing them are given in books listed in Appendix A (ii).

Some of the children who make up tunes will want to keep a record of them. They can put them on tape, but they may also be able to write them down, using numbers or the letter names engraved on most of the instruments. Some of them may be able to use tonic sol-fa or even staff notation. If they have been introduced to the hand-signs these also will help them in their notation.

Much instrumental work can be done without the reading of music, but we should be failing our children if, at some stage, we did not do all possible to help them to read simple tunes. Some of them will find this difficult; others make better progress in reading music than in reading words. Again, we may start with numbers or letter-names or even pictures: for the very backward some schools associate each chime-bar or note on a xylophone with a particular colour on a chart. Interesting and imaginative experimental work in playing the chime bars from shapes, colours, words, letters, road-signs and other objects attractive to children, has recently been done by John A. Harvey with severely retarded juniors. Some of this is now available for teachers in his two books, *Sense, Speech, and Concentration Training through Chime Bars and Visual Aids* (Paxton). All the pitch percussion instruments can be used to add colour to nursery rhymes—e.g. the tubular bells in 'Oranges and Lemons', and the glockenspiel for the mouse running up and down the clock in 'Hickory, dickory, dock'. And the teacher will find them valuable for patterning melodies, accompanying songs, playing melodic fragments for the children to echo or answer, and for stimulating or accompanying movement.

The sound of all the instruments mentioned so far is

produced by striking or tapping. Some of our children will prefer stringed instruments they can pluck. Very valuable work has been done in the making of plucked instruments by Ronald Roberts of St. Luke's College, Exeter. Basing his experiments on old instruments in museums and described in books he has designed a number of simple instruments in which each string is tuned to the note of a scale, and so is ready for playing without the finger patterns required on the orthodox or fretted string instruments. These instruments which have already proved successful in many special classes are fully described in his book, *Musical Instruments made to be played* (Dryad Press). This also suggests a variety of interesting ways in which they can be used. The majority of these are melody instruments, but at least one—the chordal dulcimer—has its strings grouped so that they form chords. The four chords which are available on it: tonic, supertonic, dominant and subdominant (d, r, s, f), make it a very suitable instrument for the accompaniment of songs as well as for use in instrumental ensembles.

All these string instruments produce satisfying sounds, and are as appropriate for use by seniors as by juniors. Some of them can be purchased; others we, and perhaps some of our pupils, can make in the craft shop to the specifications of their designer. When they are played in combination with bamboo pipes, recorders, and the pitch and rhythm percussion instruments—with all of which they sound well—we shall have to watch the balance of instruments carefully, as the sound made by the strings is comparatively small. But this quiet sound will train the children to listen more carefully and to restrain their percussive playing.

Two instruments which have been used by some

teachers to add a melodic line and a contrast of colour to percussion ensembles are the 'kazoo'—really a toy instrument, and the melodica—a simple wind instrument with a miniature piano keyboard. The kazoo has been found to help some children who have pitch difficulties in singing, and others who are shy of speaking. After playing it in an 'orchestra' children often become sufficiently interested to learn a more authentic instrument. The melodica needs quite small finger movements and good breath control. For teachers who would like to experiment with it more information can be found in *The New Melodica Tutor*, by A. W. Rowe (publisher Hohner).

The harmonica (mouth-organ) has always been a popular instrument with boys, and its popularity has recently been given a boost by its inclusion amongst the backing instruments of 'pop' and folk groups. It can be used as a solo instrument, as a member of a harmonica band or as part of a more varied ensemble. Boys' pockets are not the best places for it to be stored—and it is not quite as easy to play well as is sometimes suggested. But it has many points in its favour, not least of which is its association with out-of-door activities. A tutor has been written* which contains instructions for the teaching of both the harmonica and recorder, and exercises and excerpts which combine the two instruments and show clearly the interesting contrast of tone colours that can be obtained when they are played together.

If we intend to use the recorder we must make sure that the child who is going to play it is physically able to perform the necessary movements. Some children find considerable difficulty in making small, precise move-

* Rowe and Walters, *Harmonica and Recorder Teachers' Manual* with five pupils' books (Hohner).

ments and the holes of the descant recorder—the cheapest of the consort—may prove rather too close together for them to finger comfortably. Perhaps they can begin with notes like G and E which need not involve so much individual finger control, and for which the thumb of the right hand provides a good balance of the instrument. These notes can be integrated into the instrumental score we have arranged, and from them the children can proceed to more difficult fingerings. For quite a long time we shall avoid the lowest two notes—D and C—which need very careful breath control. For the more able players we shall begin with the three notes B A G which move down in pitch as the fingers move down the barrel of the recorder, and as the notes move down on the stave.

In teaching the position of the hands we must be sure that the children understand what we want them to do. They imitate before they adapt, and if we demonstrate hand positions facing them they will tend to do with their right hand what we are doing with our left and vice-versa. The photographs in some tutors will cause the same confusion. If our demonstration is done on a tenor recorder as we stand beside the learner the position of both our hands and fingers will be clearer.

In order to sustain the interest of the children it is important that they should be able to play tunes, however simple, on their instruments as quickly as possible, and be involved in ensemble work as soon as they can produce a clear note. Even one note can provide a rhythmic counterpoint to the main tune played by the teacher or the more able members of the group. It may surprise us to find what pleasure they get from being able to participate in this way. Possibilities increase with two notes, and as we have seen with the pitch percussion instruments, by the time the player has mastered three notes he can be playing quite interesting little tunes himself. Most tutors contain a number of three-note tunes, and for recorder players an ingenious *Suite on Three Notes* has been written by Kenneth Simpson (publisher Schott).

Some of our children are particularly attracted to the sound of the bamboo pipe—the quietness and purity of its tone appeals to them. In the making and decorating of a bamboo pipe we have another opportunity for combining music, art, and craft, and for the training of the eyes and hands as well as the ears. The tuning of the instrument demands very careful listening, and its colourful decorations provides a stimulus to the imagination. Pipes with a limited number of notes can be made, and these may be more suitable for some of our pupils than those with the full range. If it proves impossible to make the pipes in the school they can be purchased— but only as a last resort. Two books which will help teachers in the making and decorating of pipes are *The Pipers' Guild Handbook* by Margaret James (publisher Cramer), and *Making and playing bamboo pipes* by Margaret Galloway (publisher Dryad Press).

For many of our senior boys the small amount of sound produced by both pipes and recorders proves unsatisfying, and the instruments may, unfortunately, be associated in their minds with the junior department they thought they had left behind. They are very sensitive about being given activities which they consider to be childish, and, in any case they want a volume of sound more commensurate with their own size and growing sense of power—instruments which don't impose so much restraint on their blowing. For them the brass instruments are often the most acceptable

E

medium of musical expression. If they have a suitable embouchure they are likely to make much quicker progress on these than on one of the instruments of the string or woodwind family. Within a comparatively short time they can play several notes, and if we arrange our music with their achievements in mind they, too, can become members of our instrumental ensemble. Even a brass quartet is not impossible.

In some of our schools this instrumental group may well be composed of a mixed and unorthodox collection of instruments, including the tea-chest bass and combs and paper. We may also have a clarinet and guitar. The guitar has become almost a status symbol amongst boys since the proliferation of the various 'pop' groups, and has helped to make music acceptable in areas where at one time it was considered hardly a suitable male interest. The boys' desire to play the chords which they need to accompany their 'pop' and folk-songs makes them more willing to work hard to acquire the basic techniques, and to master the three chords I, IV, V. These chords can be incorporated effectively into the accompaniments to our songs and into the scores for our other instrumental combinations. We shall find that our own creative powers, as well as those of the pupils are stretched to their limits in order to provide the orchestration that the strange but exciting collection of instruments we have collected together require if their players are to be fully involved in the music-making.

All these instruments from the simplest to the most difficult make available the possibility of much more varied and interesting accompaniments to our songs than can usually be supplied by a piano. They can help to intensify the mood of the song, to illustrate its words, to portray its chief characters and to underline such of its musical features as rhythm, phrasing, and climax. They can provide short melodic or rhythmic introductions and colourful interludes between the verses. In some songs the descant we add will sound effective on a recorder or glockenspiel, in others an instrument more appropriate to the words (e.g. a cornet in 'John Peel') might be used. Other accompaniments might be based on a simple rhythmic figure (played on the castanets and tambourines in a Spanish song), a repeated melodic phrase or ostinato (played on the tubular bells or chime bars during the last verse of 'O No John'), even just a drone (on the open strings of a cello for 'The Campbells are coming'). An auto-harp could be added to the ensemble as a chordal instrument, and we might experiment with any other instruments we can find like the *mbira*, the African 'thumb piano' and the bamboo stamping tubes of the Far East—bamboo tubes of different lengths and diameters which produce pleasing sounds when struck on other bamboo or wood. As well as providing accompaniments for our songs, the instrumental ensembles can be used to accompany folk and country dancing—ballroom dancing, too, for that matter—and perhaps for P.E. displays.

In our instrumental work, as in all our other musical activities we must do everything possible to establish confidence and sustain enthusiasm. This will mean having a wide variety of instruments of different degrees of difficulty available, arranging our music with the abilities and limitations of each of the children in view, discovering how to adapt instruments to overcome physical handicaps, and at all times giving encouragement and praise to the instrumentalists whenever we see genuine effort being made, however small the results they produce.

5

Listening to Music

LISTENING is not an activity that can be limited to a separate time-table called 'Appreciation'. It is basic to all our music-making, and we can hardly expect concentrated listening from children during the time specially reserved for that purpose if their regular aural training has been neglected at other times. As has already been suggested, precise listening does not come easily to them. It demands attention, concentration, and discrimination, and against these factors their daydreaming, restlessness, and lack of vitality militate.

For all children the act of conscious, focussed listening is becoming increasingly difficult. Sound achieves its significance only in relation to silence, and this is now a rare commodity, even in country areas. In noisy towns and overcrowded houses many people are having to assume an armour of protective deafness in order to maintain an element of quietness within themselves. There is a danger that in their immurement they will miss the beautiful as well as the ugly and trivial. Other people have become so accustomed to accepting music as an accompaniment to other activities that it has lost its power of making any direct impact on them. Many of our children come from homes in which this is the case. Somehow we have to train them to become alive to sounds, and then to become selective and discriminating. This process of selecting amongst so many

sounds is not easy for slow learners, and without encouragement and guidance they will lack the motiva-
tion and lose the will to make the necessary effort. But
when their interest and enthusiasm have been aroused
they will be just as responsive to the music we play to
them as other children—sometimes more so, because
they are not insulated from it by an outer covering of
sophistication.

This training in *listening* (as contrasted with hearing
or over-hearing) will begin on the day the children enter
the school, and its effect will be felt in all their other
activities as well as in their music. If it is neglected their
understanding of the world around them will suffer, and
even their capacity as wage-earners may be affected.

The first step towards directed conscious listening
comes with an awareness of silence, and then of the
sound that grows out of the silence. This may be just an
everyday sound which the children can hear in the
room, or a special musical sound which has been made
by the striking of a chime bar or by the plucking of a
cello string, with nothing else to distract attention from
it. The second step involves a discrimination between
sounds, and then an appreciation of their different
qualities.

For the child who comes to us from a musical home
this training will already have begun. As a baby he
will have heard his mother singing to him, and he may
also have had melodies played to him on such instruments as a dulcimer, a bamboo pipe or even a lyre.
Other children, who have missed these musical experiences, may have had their attention directed to natural
sounds like the songs of birds,* the soughing of the wind

* An excellent record of bird song is *A Tapestry of British Bird Song*
(CLP 1723).

in the trees, and the rippling of the brook. ('Look at . . .', however, is still a more common expression than 'Listen to . . .'). In our towns their attention may have been drawn to other sounds—the ringing of church bells, the occasional barrel organ, the cry of the paper sellers. Or they may have heard a variety of sounds, musical and non-musical, in the BBC's pre-school programme 'Listen with Mother', or on gramophone records.

Inevitably our children will come to school with differing backgrounds of awareness to sounds, and we shall probably find that the majority of the slow learners have been less fortunate in this respect than their friends. We must do all possible to extend their horizons by introducing them to a wide range of stimulating aural experiences.

Let us begin by encouraging them to experiment with the sounds that can be made by using quite simple materials and substances—e.g. sounds produced by the shaking of rice, dried peas or small shells in various types of containers, the twanging of elastic bands of different tensions, and the striking of various surfaces, including bottles filled with different amounts of liquid. Let us also use the pitch and rhythmic percussion instruments that were described in the previous chapter, blowing instruments, the piano in all its registers, and such mementoes of continental holidays as cowbells and musical boxes. Some of this exploration of sounds will be done during the time set apart for music, but there should be opportunities for the children themselves to experiment in their own free time with the instruments that are kept in the school's Music Corner or on open shelves. In this way they will be able to discover some of the exciting sounds that are possible, and the effects different sounds have on them.

We shall use our musical instruments and other sound producers, too, to illustrate and provide appropriate background effects for the stories we tell and the plays the children act. We may try to imitate actual sounds, e.g. the ringing of the alarm clock that wakes us up, or we may create an atmosphere—e.g. the eery sounds that greet the spacemen as they step out of their ship to explore the planet on which they have just landed. We shall play to our children gramophone records and tapes of domestic and out-of-doors sounds that they meet regularly, and of some strange ones with which they are less familiar, so that they can incorporate these, too, in their stories and poems. (See Appendix C (i).)

Gradually they will move from this rudimentary awareness of various sounds to a stage when they begin to compare and contrast them—the loud and the soft, the big and the small, the high and the low, the dark and the bright, the silky and the velvety. They will have their own original ways of describing them, and this will be done in less abstract language than that used by other children. After the extremes will come discrimination between the less clearly defined gradations in between. In this process hand, arm, and body movements from the children, and visual aids provided by the teacher will be of more help than words towards a clearer understanding of the concept of pitch.

Much of the training in listening described so far has been concerned with pitch, texture, and intensity. There must be a corresponding rhythmic training. Short rhythmic groups can be tapped out for the children to tap back and contrasted pieces—marches, waltzes, etc. —played for them to beat time to. Or we can speak names and word patterns for them to imitate, remembering that some of them will find the co-ordination of hand movements difficult, and others will have greater difficulty with speech. The use of the children's own names and those of well-known people, places, and things will simplify the process of memorization and establish confidence. In these early stages our aim is not so much to secure complete accuracy of reproduction as to encourage habits of concentrated listening. Other rhythmic training through the sort of percussion work suggested in the previous chapter will also help towards this end.

When the children have learnt a number of songs we could try out a musical game on the lines of that described by Cyril Winn in his book *Teaching Music* (OUP), p. 85. The titles of the songs or appropriate phrases from them are played on the piano, and by recognizing them the children can complete the story. This is the story he gives:

' "Early One Morning" "Daisy" was walking along the "Banks of Loch Lomond", and, looking up, she saw a "Tit Willow" flying "Over the Sea to Skye". This reminded her of her brother in the R.A.F., and she thought to herself, "My Bonnie is over the Ocean". In the distance she heard someone whistling "She'll be coming round the mountain", and as she came nearer she saw it was her old friend "John Peel"; but they could not remember the last time they met. She thought, romantically of course, "Somewhere over the rainbow", he, more practical, thought "On Ilkla' Moor". Presently they got engrossed in conversation, and he said to her, "I will give my Love an Apple", but she said to him, "Drink to me only", but he replied, "I want something more thirst-quenching. There must be 'A Tavern in the Town' somewhere." "Yes," she said, "there's 'The Mermaid'." Here they refreshed themselves and spent the rest of the day with "The Old Folks at Home".'

The songs we use will vary according to the age and ability of the group, and any 'pop' numbers or radio hits we introduce will have to be kept right up-to-date. It is not always easy to fix a name to a tune we know, and our children may find it very difficult. But if a spark of recognition appears in their eyes we can be satisfied that they have been listening carefully to our playing, and we can probably produce the necessary title as a communal effort.

At a later stage our classes may enjoy discovering 'hidden tunes'. These are well-known song or hymn tunes played on the piano, but not always in the more usual place—on the top. Sometimes they are hidden in the bass and sometimes in the middle, decorated by other tunes. Two good collections of these have been made by Geoffrey Shaw.* They are not easy to play, and the arrangements need practice if we are to avoid over-emphasizing, or losing altogether the main tune. If our own keyboard technique is not adequate, perhaps we can persuade a pianist friend to record them on tape for us.

Another musical 'game' might be the recognition and naming of instruments with which the children have already experimented. With eyes closed they will see if they can distinguish between the tambourine and the triangle, the chime bar and the chordal dulcimer, the drum and the castanet—some instruments very different in sound, some more alike. Later this can be extended to include the instruments of the orchestra—at first using instruments which are clearly contrasted in pitch or texture, e.g. the flute and the cello, the trumpet and the harp, and only later when the children's power of discrimination has increased, asking them to distinguish

* *Hidden Tunes*, Books I and II (Nelson).

between the clarinet and the bassoon or the trumpet and the trombone. In certain registers some instruments within a family are not easy to tell apart even by quite experienced listeners, and the introduction of instruments in their families is not particularly helpful for our children, whatever may be its value to others. The set of records *Tunes for Children** arranged by Roger Fiske will prove useful for demonstrating the characters of contrasted instruments playing together. The pitch and texture of voices should also be introduced in the first instance through their extremes: an advanced stage of listening is required to distinguish between a mezzo-soprano and an alto.

The basic aural training involved in all these activities will help our children to enjoy more fully any music we play to them during the time that is reserved specifically for listening.

Even more than other children, they get greater benefit from live music played to them by a performer in the classroom than from music coming out of a gramophone or radio. The personality of the performer helps to integrate them as a listening group, and the visual aspect of the performance aids their concentration. Their concentration may be on the movements of the performer and the construction of the instrument at first, but this, for many children, leads on to an interest in the music being performed—especially when the performer is a person they know and like. So let us sing and play to our group as often as possible. Perhaps we can play the treble recorder or the guitar, and the music chosen need not be difficult. Some recent television programmes have helped to revive an interest in the piano, and teachers who can play simple piano

* H.M.V. 7EG 8575-6.

pieces competently are often greeted by the highest form of praise known to a child: 'Oh, Miss, you ought to be on the telly'. Short pieces must be chosen at first: often 30-40 seconds is long enough to begin with, and this time can gradually be extended.

In Secondary Schools we shall probably find quite an amount of hidden performing talent in other classes to help us out—pianists, guitarists, clarinettists who play in a jazz group, and brass instrumentalists from local uniformed organizations. When we have exhausted all the possibilities amongst the staff, parents, and other pupils, perhaps we can invite a visiting performer to come and play to the children. If so, we must make sure that the visitor understands their special needs and is able to establish friendly relations with them. It is easy —but disastrous—for him to overestimate their listening capacity, or at the opposite extreme to talk down to what he considers to be their level.

The instrumentalist who has accurately assessed the situation can stimulate the interest and hold the atten-attention of the group by a variety of means. He will be alive to the sense of curiosity and expectation that can be aroused as he deliberately opens his instrument case, takes out the various parts of his instrument (if, for example, it is a flute or a clarinet) and fits them to-gether. If he plays a string instrument he will make a point of tuning it in the presence of the children, and he will point out a few salient features of its construction. When he begins to play he will position himself so that the movements of his fingers and of the bow across the strings can be seen by all. These movements will be clearest on a fairly large instrument that is held in front of the performer's body. It is important, too, to think about the range of pitch of the instrument, remembering that high frequencies can make some children very tense.

A cello obviously answers all these demands, and outstanding work has been done on this instrument with groups of children, from the 'ineducable' in Training Centres to the slow learners in ordinary schools, by Miss Juliette Alvin. She describes her approach and techniques in Chapter 5 of her recent book *Music for the Handicapped Child* (OUP). Great emphasis is placed on the need for the instrumentalist to become well acquainted with the school and its pupils so that she can select the type of music that is likely to make an appeal, and estimate the length of time the children can be expected to listen. (This depends not only on the children's ability, but on their previous experience and training.) There should be an opportunity for the visitor to discuss her work with the full-time members of staff, and these should all attend the programme, if possible, so that they can relate it to the children's general activities. Whatever the length of the programme, at some point the children should be actively involved in it, by tapping quietly, by miming, or by humming and singing melodies which are familiar to them. It is important to include some familiar item in every programme.

A gramophone record rarely sustains the attention of the group as long or as effectively as a performer in the classroom, but if used judiciously as an aid it has its own special contribution to make. It should go without saying that all the equipment must be of the best quality available, and that the amplification must produce sufficient volume for the children to listen without strain. Normal children become restless when they have to exert themselves to listen to a record: our children

will give up altogether. The effectiveness of the reproduction depends to a large extent on the position of the
gramophone or loudspeaker. It should be so placed that
all the children can be seated near to the source of
sound in a reasonably comfortable manner. In the
early stages our children may want an amount of
volume that the teacher would consider deafening: the
loudness provides them with a sense of security—they
can lose themselves in it. We must be careful not to
snatch this security from them too suddenly. For most
groups quite a short section from a record will be
sufficient, and as it is not easy to isolate just the required
amount on an LP or EP, it will be a help if the teacher
can tape various extracts of the lengths she considers
suitable for her particular group. In any case, the
gramophone has lost some of its immediate glamour,
and the mechanism of the tape-recorder is more likely to
attract spontaneous interest.

Many children enjoy music which paints a picture or
tells a story. Our children are often not particularly
interested in the picture or story that was in the com-
poser's mind, and prefer to imagine their own. And
why not? Music conjuring up pictures of breaking
waves or storms at sea have little meaning for children
who have never been to the seaside (and there are still
some of these), or for 'trippers' whose visits extend no
farther than the amusement pavilion on the pier or the
fish-and-chip shops. The teacher needs great skill in her
descriptions and frequent reference to pictures and
sounds if she is to evoke the intended atmosphere. She
may also be able to use film strips and link up the listening with current television programmes. But if the
children are getting pleasure from the colourful orchestration, there is no need for disappointment if they are

imagining another scene altogether. Imagination can be stunted as well as stimulated by description and pictorial 'aids'.

Some music which tells a story, like *The Sorcerer's Apprentice*, loses its full meaning unless the main events of the story are known. These will be clearer to the children if pictures can be used, in books, on the blackboard or flannelgraph, or projected on to a screen. The stories must be fairly short and uncomplicated, without too many characters. *Peter and the Wolf*, although not a long story, lasts a long time and has many characters with their associated instruments to be remembered. Miming, acting, and again, pictures may help here—as also in *The Carnival of the Animals*—to aid continuity and concentration. If the main purpose of a story is to direct attention to one particular instrument, a record like *Tubby the Tuba* will be more successful. An occasional word from the teacher during the playing will help to highlight important features and bring back wandering attention, but anything in the nature of a running commentary should be avoided.

Although the extra-musical features may encourage concentrated listening in some children, one gets constant surprises, and often it is, in fact, abstract music with a clear-cut formal structure and recurrent rhythmic patterns that children ask for. They enjoy its neatness and sense of inevitability. Chopin's Prelude in A Major, with its crisp, repeated rhythm ♩ ♪♫♩ ♩ ♩ and the sequential structure of its melody has often proved a winner: so has the rondo of Haydn's Trumpet Concerto, with its easily recognizable solo instrument and repeated melodic and rhythmic patterns. Our children get confused by the mass of sound produced by

a full orchestra, and a solo instrument standing out
clearly from this acts as a focus for their listening. Here
again, a picture of the solo instrument* or better still the
instrument itself for the children to handle, should be
introduced wherever possible. Perhaps, too, the children
could mime the playing of the instrument when it
makes its appearance.

We shall find that much recent music speaks in a
more understandable language to our children than it
does to many adults: Stravinsky and Bartók are often
quite firm favourites.

There will, of course, be a number of children who
for reasons of background, experience, and tempera-
ment will show no spontaneous interest in the type of
music loosely called 'classical'. Although we should not
give up our efforts with them too early (we have seen
how they like music which is familiar to them), we may
have to find a starting point within their own experience. This may be the signature tunes and background
music of television serials they watch regularly—e.g.
'Johnny Todd', the Z Cars signature tune which is also
a folk-song, can lead to a variety of musical activities. It
may be the 'pop' records which their brothers and sisters
play incessantly at home.

About our own attitude to 'pop' we must be quite
clear, especially in Secondary Schools. We can pretend
it doesn't exist. We can recognize its existence, but
refuse to admit it into our schools. We can recognize
that it already exists in our schools, whether we want it
there or not—if only in the heads of the pupils—and see
what we can do to develop discrimination amongst the
hits figuring in the charts. We can, perhaps, help its

* Large pictures of the instruments are available from Boosey &
Hawkes.

devotees to discover that it is only a small part of the whole world of music waiting to be explored. Whatever the attitude we adopt, let us be positive in our approach and not condescending. In this way we are more likely to win the respect of our pupils than by weakly compromising and agreeing (with a hint of bribery) that we will listen to one of their records if they will listen to one of ours.

One lesson we can all learn from the children's devotion to their 'pop' heroes is that the music they will accept depends far more upon their attraction to the performer than to the music he is performing. If they like us they will be more prepared to consider whatever type of music we introduce to them than if we label ourselves as squares at their first meeting with us. Let us remember, too, that the 'boy next door' who makes good is a person with whom many of our children want to identify themselves for emotional reasons.

All of us, adults as well as children, find it quite difficult to give our undivided attention to a piece of music for long—especially if it is completely new, unless there are landmarks we can move towards and signposts to guide us on the way. Before our children listen to an orchestral work it is wise for them to be introduced to the more important of these landmarks. The main themes can be played to them on the piano or a melodic instrument, and they may be able to sing, whistle, or play some of them themselves. They can then join in quietly humming when their tune makes it appearance, and the music, because of its familiarity, will have added meaning for them. With a favourite tune to wait for, they will often be prepared to listen to quite a lot that goes on before its appearance—and absorb much of it subconsciously. They can also learn the characteristic rhythmic figures that occur frequently, so that they can tap these quietly when they hear them. Sometimes a whole movement is based on such a rhythm—e.g. the Pavane from Peter Warlock's *Capriol Suite*, which has this rhythm ♩♫ played throughout it.

The percussion instruments can be used as an aid to listening, provided, of course, that they don't obliterate the music they are meant to be accompanying. The more skeletal the texture of the percussion score, the better the listening will be. Cyril Winn* tells how an 'A' stream and a 'D' stream in a north-country city Secondary School both listened to Chopin's Polonaise in A Major. The 'D' stream played a simple percussion band arrangement as they listened, the 'A' stream *just* listened. After three lessons the two classes were asked to whistle the middle section. The 'D' stream did so with surprising accuracy: the 'A' stream were unable to reproduce any section at all.

We may find that some of our senior classes are able to follow such simple scores as the Larg's Single-Stave Guides.† These have only one stave to be followed, and on this the chief melodies and rhythms are written with the instruments which play them clearly indicated. Some senior classes have found the Tonescript Charts‡ helpful for focusing attention. On these each instrument is represented by a colour, and from the groupings of the colours and the patterns they make the children can follow the main melodies and recognize the places where the full orchestra plays. As well as aiding concentration, the charts may help to give some children an

* *Teaching Music,* p. 55.

† Published by Larg & Sons (Dundee) Ltd., Whitehall Street, Dundee.

‡ Tonescript Productions Ltd., 3 Village Way, Sanderstead, Surrey.
F

insight into orchestration. These charts are designed for individual use, but with our children it will be helpful if, in the first instance, a master chart is used at the front of the class which they can all see, and on which the teacher can point out the various patterns the music is making as it is being played. There are 'colourgraphs' available in film strip form of the 'Nutcracker' Suite, and the overtures *Fingal's Cave*, *A Midsummer Night's Dream* and *The Barber of Seville*.*

Other children listen with greatest concentration during a movement period, where they are required to vary their movements according to the changing tempo, volume, intensity, and pitch of the music (see Chapter 6).

After its first introduction to the class, a piece of music should be repeated frequently so that the children can become familiar with it. This need not be during the regular music period. The piece may, for example, be suitable to be played before the morning Act of Worship when the whole school is seated quietly in the Hall, and an orchestral piece like *Vltava* could make its re-appearance during a travel talk about Czechoslovakia.

We should always beware of expecting from our groups the response we ourselves made when we first heard it, or that we now make after hearing it many times. Sometimes the child may show greater insight than those of us who teach him, and for whom the freshness of the music's appeal has gone. He may not wish to put into words what he is feeling. He may prefer to express it through painting or movement—or just cherish it in himself. Let us respect his reticence.

The radio has not been mentioned. It is a valuable

* Tonescript Productions Ltd., 3 Village Way, Sanderstead, Surrey.

additional aid if its programme can be integrated with the work we have prepared—but it can never be used as an alternative to it. Most of the music broadcasts for schools move too quickly for our children, but we may be able to use parts of 'The Music Box' for juniors, and 'Adventures in Music' for seniors. For this latter series the pamphlets are essential, with their excellent pictures to stimulate and focus the interest of the children. In fact it would be worth buying a stock of these pamphlets for their pictures alone. They may also suggest new ideas to us for incorporation in our own lessons. All that has been said about the quality of the gramophone equipment and the positioning of the amplifier applies with equal force to the radio—and the radio controls must be in the same room as the music teacher.

Various records and a number of film-strips which it is hoped the children will enjoy are listed in Appendices C (iv) and D.

6

Movement and Dance
by Miss V. Bruce

THIS chapter is concerned with the contribution which movement and dance can make to the musical education of children who find learning difficult.

Movement is a very good medium of expression for all children, but especially for the slow learner because it is one in which everybody can take part from the first in an expressive and creative way. There is no competition. Nobody will spoil the work by moving less well. Each child can work at his own level to a great extent, gaining some degree of success in his achievement, however limited it may be. This depends, of course, upon a teacher who knows how to guide whilst leaving scope for each individual, and how to accept and use movement ideas which the children may have without encroaching insensitively with her own preconceptions about what the movement should look like.

In a movement class all children can participate at one time. No one is waiting for a turn. No equipment is necessary in the first place: all that is required is a space. This unfortunately is so often hard to come by, but even quite a small space like a cleared classroom offers some opportunity. Soon it is necessary to introduce percussion instruments and music, but movement, dance, and dance drama can develop for some time with only the use of the body, the teacher's voice, and such noises as can be made using the voices of the children and percussive noises with hands and feet on the floor or with hands on the body.

Movement training, then, can begin before a class has started to use instruments—even before the materials necessary for percussive and other musical activities have arrived in the school, and it can continue developing gradually into the art of the dance, and as an art which can help the general education of the children. It is this latter aspect of the work on which we shall concentrate in this chapter.

The qualities of movement are also those of sound. One can be strong—hitting, thrusting, pressing, pulling, exerting one's power. One can be light and delicate, touching the ground and the air finely or gently. One can be heavy, drooping, falling with the burden of weight. Movement can be sudden, fleeting, flying, darting, jerky, and it can be slow, calm, steady, and smooth. Movement can be big, broad, taking up much space, or it can be narrow and closed in, squeezed into little space.

These qualities are also found in sound. The drum can be strong, loud, and firm, as can the trumpet. Bells are often light and delicate, can be the violin, the piccolo, and the flute. A drum slack in tension can be heavy and deep, as can a bassoon and the sound of feet dragging along the floor and the body falling on to the floor. Music can make sharp, jerky, percussive sounds—e.g. notes played staccato on the piano and pizzicato on strings, or a stick hitting sharply on the side of the drum. Music can be smooth and calm—e.g. the legato playing of the violin, viola, or cello. A gong can ring out, long lasting, diminishing in sound but smooth. Sound can be broad and big—e.g. widely spaced chords on a piano, the spacious sound of brass, the soaring melody of strings. Sound can be narrow—e.g. notes close together, hands crossing one another on the piano, the high pitch of the piccolo or descant recorder, the small sounds of wooden blocks and clappers. Sound can be lovely, finished, harmonious like the ringing of a gong, or it can be harsh and distorted like cymbals clashing or a pair of hands descending at random on to a piano keyboard. Movement can also be like this—the body moving harmoniously with all its parts working in co-operation; or twisting distorting grotesquely, the parts moving against one another.

In all these ways movement and music can be linked together. The quality of movement brings an understanding to the children of the meaning of strong, light, quick, smooth, etc., so that in turn they can understand these qualities in sound and music. Music can be used to accompany movement or to act as its stimulus, so that the children become aware of the relationship between the quality of the music and the quality of their movement. This awareness develops in them a greater sensitivity to music as they listen and perform, and helps them to a better understanding of it.

There is also the whole area of time, rhythm, and phrasing to be explored through movement. Children in classes for the slow learners sometimes find movement in partnership with an outside rhythm difficult. They must first discover their own rhythms. There is always a place, especially in the early days, for movement which is left without any musical sound so that the children can use their own individual rhythms, e.g.

'Fill up the room, go everywhere, but go as quickly or as slowly as you like.'

Children are very individual in their ability to conform to imposed rhythms, and one must allow development to take place in some of them very slowly. The body is essentially rhythmic, and most children soon begin to experience pulse and accent through their bodies, marking them with gesture in different parts of the body and with steps. Unfortunately, one often sees the children's rhythmic response through music confined to stepping, when really children can respond so much more fully if they are allowed and encouraged to use many parts of the body—hands, head, elbows, feet, the middle of the body, etc.

By an extension of this rhythmic training we can help to bring children to an understanding of musical rhythm, note values, and phrasing through locomotion and through gesture.

Movement can help children to feel the pulse of the music and to hear the melody. For instance, they can dance the tune up in the air using their arms and heads, and then mark the beat with steps and jumps, or they can choose which part of the tune they would like to dance. The part which movement can play in helping children to come to terms with rhythm and quality in music is one of its most valuable features, especially for backward children, for whom movement is a fairly ready language. The conductor of an orchestra is, after all, a dancer in essence.

Stillness is very important, especially for the children we are considering who are so often excitable, emotionally stirred, and physically restless. Movement and dance can greatly assist the training of stillness—the awareness of the body as a still thing, e.g. the statue, or of the body lying still, resting. The dance or movement sequence must always have a clear beginning and a clear end, as has the sound of music. This training is important, too, for getting the right attitude and preparation for listening, for the training of relaxation. I often start and finish my lessons with a difficult class with listening, whilst they lie, still and relaxed.

There is a dance 'rule' which I make in all my classes, however simple the work may be: it is that no dancer must move from the last position he had taken until the 'lady at the piano' lifts the pedal or the sound stops. In this way children really learn to listen to the end, and finish their dancing clearly and musically.

Making music with percussion instruments plays a prominent part in the musical education of our children. They can discover the quality of percussive sound, often dancing with an instrument such as a drum, small cymbals, bells, etc. Some children can play instruments for others to dance to, accompanying the movements of the dancers. Sound can be both a stimulus and an accompaniment to movement. As a partner for children's movement and dancing, percussive sound is very good because it is simple, because the children can handle the instruments themselves and because the sounds produced can be so varied. Melodic instruments like recorders and simple string instruments can also be a very good accompaniment and stimulus for movement. The child can, in turn, be player and dancer.

By making dances and dance dramas to music, however simple, children learn to listen carefully and to know the music that is being played, music which they almost 'own' when they hear it on television and radio. So it is important to choose music of quality which has borne the test of time as well as the 'pop' record with the persistent beat. One can never, it seems, come to decisive conclusions about the children's own choice of music, or what they can listen to. Often they enjoy music which we might consider too difficult—e.g Ibert's *Divertissements*, Vaughan Williams's *Job* (*Satan's Dance of Triumph*), Saint-Saëns' *The Swan*. I have found backward children who not only get pleasure from such music but really seem to react sensitively to it. So one can hope that it will be possible from time to time to use really fine orchestral music for dance exploration.

Dance drama sometimes calls for 'mood music' which can help children with atmosphere and sometimes with the shape of the dance, e.g. a child knows that he comes in with the loud part of the music. The music supplies the 'landmarks' and helps children to memorise the complete pattern of the dance drama. This, again, provides opportunities for children to come to know music and to love it.

The part to be played by dance in the helping of backward children to learn and love music is a large one. All arts are very important in the education of our children, and all of them are to some degree interdependent. Dance and music can be independent arts, but dance often requires the partnership of music, and in the work briefly described here it can greatly help to open up the whole realm of music to our children. It can do this with reasonable success, sometimes with astonishing success, and without the frustration which they experience so often in their other activities.

The list of books and music given in the Appendices will, it is hoped, encourage teachers to begin their own experiments, and so enable them to prove this for themselves.

7

The Relation of Music to other Subjects

THROUGHOUT this book emphasis has been placed on music as an integral part of a child's whole education, not just one of several isolated subjects which the child himself is expected to relate to each other and synthesize into a unified, meaningful learning experience. Our children are not capable of such an intellectual exercise: how many children are? Music will not be presented to them as a neatly sellotaped parcel to be opened when one bell rings and tightly stuck up again at the sound of another; nor, presumably, will geography, history, or any of the other 'subjects'. The children must be helped to see the relationships of their various activities as they participate in them, and to understand them as different but complementary methods of exploring life—their own life and the lives of other people.

From some of their songs they can learn a considerable amount about people and places in other parts of the world, and as they discover new countries in their travel lessons they will be able to learn the songs that the people who live in them sing. From other songs they can learn about what happened in the past, and what is happening in the history that is being made at present; and as they delve back in time and learn about the lives of people in other ages, they can also learn about the sort of musical instruments those people played, and the kind of dances with which they entertained themselves.

Let us look at this aspect of our teaching in a little more detail. Every country, and usually every region within a country, has its own songs—its folk and national songs, and perhaps songs by composers who lived there. The folk and national songs, especially, tell us in their words about the life, scenery, occupations and traditions of their country, and their music often evokes its atmosphere better than words can do. Our descriptions of the lives of the people of Norway and Spain, for example, will be greatly helped by a careful choice of songs from those countries.

We live on an island, and so a large number of our own traditional songs are associated with the sea—about sailors leaving their sweethearts and families to go away to sea ('Johnny Todd' and 'Swansea Town'), and about the voyages they made and the ports at which their ships called ('Spanish Ladies' and 'Donkey Riding'). A large globe would be useful for tracing these voyages. Perhaps some of the songs could be acted, with the sailors being greeted at the ports by children dressed in the national costume of the country. This would give our groups an opportunity to draw pictures and make models of the produce of the country, and perhaps to hear some of its traditional music and poetry. As the sailors go on their voyages there are shanties for them to sing at their work, and plenty of good physical exercise in the pulling, hauling and turning movements that the shanties were designed to help. Other songs connected with the sea tell the story of our fishing trade, and the risks the fishermen have to take to bring their catch safely back to us ('Caller Herrin').

There are many songs about the work of country people on the land, and the industrial areas have songs which are based on events related to the local industries. The children may get pleasure finding songs which belong to their own locality, or which refer to their town or region and the people who lived there—'Kelvin Grove', the 'Sussex Carol', 'Scarborough Fair,' 'Men of Harlech', 'The Wee Cooper o' Fife', 'John Peel'.

From the United States come the songs of the cowboys and the rounding up of the cattle ('The Lone Star Trail', 'Git along little Dogies'), the spirituals with their insights into the hard lives of the negroes, and a large number of other songs like 'The Ballad of the Tea Party' which deal with incidents from American history.

Every country has its own songs about the customs, pleasures and occupations of its people—'The Girl who Loved Dancing' (Swedish), 'Playing Giants' (Icelandic), 'The Cowkeeper's Song' (Norwegian), and 'Andulko, the Goose Girl' (Czechoslovakian). Many of the Central European songs are based on national dances—e.g. the Czech song, 'I sowed barley in the meadow' is in Polka rhythm, and it would be fun for the children to learn the steps of these dances and to dress up in the appropriate costume to perform them. This would involve co-operation with the needlework department in the Secondary School—and perhaps the P.E. department, too.

Well-known rivers of the world are featured in song— the Volga, the Arkenshaw, and Swanee Rivers (actually spelt Arkansas and Suwannee), the Missouri, and of course Old Father Thames. Some of them are portrayed in orchestral music—e.g. *Vltava* by Smetana and *The Blue Danube* by Johann Strauss. Appropriate orchestral music can often be linked up with the songs the children sing—a Hebridean song might be followed by *Fingal's Cave* Overture of Mendelssohn, a Czech folk-song by the Furiant from Smetana's opera, *The Bartered Bride*, a Spanish song by the *Spanish Dances* of Granados, and a Finnish folk-song by an extract from Sibelius's *Finlandia*.

Relevant slides and travel films could be shown, and the children could be encouraged to paint their own impressions of the countries to which their musical tour takes them, make up poems and stories about them, act from their legends or from the everyday happenings of the children who live there, and compile scrap-books of relevant illustrated material. Travel agencies may oblige by providing some colourful brochures for this purpose.

Senior pupils are likely to be more interested in the contemporary fashions of a country than in its traditional costumes. Italian and Spanish stylings and Cuban-heeled boots have been popular with young males for some years—but how many of their wearers have been able to whistle any tunes from the countries responsible for these styles? And from how many of the countries represented in their stamp collections can keen young philatelists sing a song? Yet there is a wealth of European and American singing material available, and the small collection *East West Songs** will help us in our search for simple and singable material from Africa and the East. Might it even be possible for a typical dish from the countries about which the children are singing to be prepared for or by them on a special occasion? That would involve yet another school department.

* Published for International Voluntary Work Camps by Cooperative Recreation Service Inc. at Delaware, Ohio, U.S.A.

Through their words our songs form a close link with poetry and drama. Much orchestral music is related to literature, too—either inspired by it, or designed to accompany it. An obvious example is the incidental orchestral music and songs for Shakespeare's plays. Very few of our children are likely to be able to read or follow these plays in any detail, but some of the easier incidental music written by Mendelssohn for *A Midsummer Night's Dream* may form an attractive introduction or background to the story of that play, and this, in turn, may lead on to an interest in other Shakespeare stories and to the period in which they were written with its costumes, sports, dances, and architecture. At a different level, what about some of the music from the current musicals *Oliver* and *Pickwick* as an introduction to two of Dickens's most popular characters?

Now let us turn to history. Many well-known songs are based on historical events. Some of these (e.g. 'The Vicar of Bray') have too complicated a story for our children to understand, but others with less-involved plots may help to awaken their interest in important and colourful characters from the past—e.g. 'The Skye Boat Song' will introduce them to Bonny Prince Charlie and Flora Macdonald, and 'Boney was a Warrior' to Napoleon Buonaparte. '*The Titanic*' will bring them up to more recent times, and they can be right up to date with the ballads being written about contemporary events. These songs often give a truer account of what really happened than the history books. The books, for example, tell us the basic fact that men were being 'pressed' to fight in the Napoleonic Wars: 'High Germany' tells us what this means in terms of personal feeling to a girl whose sweetheart was one of the young men to be conscripted.

The *1812 Overture* of Tchaikovsky makes another link with Napoleon, and extracts from Vaughan Williams's *Sinfonia Antartica* will bring into the classroom some of the atmosphere of the frozen expanses through which Scott travelled to the South Pole, and perhaps a greater realization of the heroism of the members of his expedition.

Another aspect of history comes alive in the minuets, gavottes, and other dances which can be played to the children; and a visit to a museum like the Victoria and Albert will enable them to see the type of instruments on which these were first played, and the style of costumes that were worn by the dancers and instrumentalists. Some of these will already be familiar to keen television viewers.

The relations between music and the visual arts is very close. After being emotionally stirred by music some children may want to express themselves through painting, drawing or modelling. Or having looked at a picture and been similarly roused, they may want to express themselves through song or even through simple vocal or instrumental improvisations. Some senior pupils may, with our help, be able to see something of the connection between the structure of the pictures at which they have been looking, and the music to which they listen.

For younger children there are many traditional songs which can be related to nature study—songs about about flowers, trees, animals, birds, insects, and the seasons of the year, and a number of songs have been written on the same subjects—e.g. the three volumes of *Nature Songs* by Martin Shaw (Cramer), are about animals, birds, and insects. Some orchestral music, too, portrays animals and birds in sound. Probably the best-known is *The Carnival of the Animals*, by Saint-Saëns, but other extracts equally attractive are Nielson's *Dance of the Cockerels*, and Tchaikovsky's *The Two Cats* (from *The Sleeping Beauty*). See also Appendix C (iv).

Many Religious Education lessons would be enlivened by the introductions of songs, hymns, carols and spirituals based on the stories that are being told, and the atmosphere of the Bible lands can be made more real by the playing of their traditional music. Some of our well-known hymns express quite simply profound truths—they are an excellent medium for teaching— and the addition of attractive, good tunes often help to illuminate their meaning. Some special schools have found that their children enjoy singing the psalms in the settings by Gelineau* (the antiphons of which can be learnt very quickly), and are able to understand and remember the words better as a result of singing them.

We have grown so accustomed to associating carols with Christmas that we tend to forget, or neglect, the carols for Lent, Passiontide, Easter, Ascension, and Whitsun. These are all carefully classified according to their appropriate Christian season in the *Oxford Book of Carols*, and in the same book there are also carols for the four seasons of the year and for harvest. Many carols were originally ring dances, and they can still be used in that way—unaccompanied, or with the accompaniment of the children's own instruments.

Orchestral music can be played to help set the scenes for some of the great events of the Bible. The 'Pastoral Symphony' from *Messiah* or the Symphony from Bach's *Christmas Oratorio* may help some children to imagine more vividly the quiet fields near Bethlehem where the shepherds were keeping watch over their sheep, and

* Joseph Gelineau, *Psalms* (Grail Publications).

there are sections of *Noye's Fludde* by Benjamin Britten which provide a dramatic background for that Old Testament story. In addition to what we can do in the R.E. lesson, we have an excellent opportunity in the daily morning assembly to combine vocal and instrumental music, poetry, mime, drama, movement and the visual arts in a concerted act of worship.

At the beginning of this century it was quite common practice for the pence-table, as well as other facts and figures, to be sung to well-known tunes as an aid to their memorization. The following verse was fitted to the tune of 'The Ash Grove':

> Twelve pence make one shilling,
> Eighteen pence one and sixpence,
> Twenty pence one and eightpence,
> Twenty-four pence two shillings.

This practice has been discontinued! But there are a number of songs which can help our children in their counting—even if they can sing only one word in them —the number word 'one', 'two', 'three', etc.: 'One man went to mow', 'One man shall mow my meadow', 'Ten Green Bottles', 'Green Grow the Rushes Oh,' 'The Seven Joys of Mary', 'This Old Man', 'The Twelve Days of Christmas,' 'Ould John Braddlum'. They will also get practice in counting during their percussion work, and in their instrumental ensembles.

By using simple material and instruments—blowing through and over tubes, experimenting with rubber bands, taut string, and stretched skin, etc., it may be possible to interest some of the senior pupils in the elementary principles of acoustics. The making of bamboo pipes and the other instruments described in Chapter Four will train their precision in measurement

G

and skill in the use of tools, and will, incidentally, take music into the craft shop. A teacher who is gifted manually and mechanically can perhaps satisfy the enquiring minds of other senior children who want to know how things are made by dismantling musical instruments and putting them together again. In the process a lot will be learnt about the construction of the instruments, more information about acoustics will emerge, and there will be opportunities for some listening. One school has already had its piano, gramophone, and tape-recorder in pieces, and the music master is now waiting with some trepidation for the day when one of his boys arrives at school with a 32-ft. flue pipe from the local church organ—removed in the interests of education.

The close connection between music and movement has been discussed in the previous chapter. It can find practical application in the Secondary School in the dancing class organized to prepare the older pupils to take their place without embarrassment in the social events of their own school and the youth clubs of the neighbourhood. This is very valuable social training for them, and the fact that they can join in the dancing on equal terms with their friends from other streams and classes gives them a satisfying sense of achievement, and a renewal of self-respect.

For the imaginative teacher the possibilities of making music meaningful in its relationship with other aspects of knowledge and of life are almost endless. Since it is a universal medium of expression for the joys, sorrows, hopes, fears, aspirations, and worshipful feelings of mankind, it is natural that it should permeate our every-day activities—mental, physical, and spiritual—and be a unifying element amongst those 'subjects' by which these are represented on our school's time-table.

Appendices

APPENDIX A

(i) General Background Reading

Slow Learners at School	Education Pamphlet No. 46	H.M.S.O.
The Education of Slow Learning Children	A. E. Tansley & R. Gulliford	Routledge
Teaching the Slow Learner in the Special School	ed. M. F. Cleugh	Methuen
Teaching the Slow Learner in the Primary School	ed. M. F. Cleugh	Methuen
Teaching the Slow Learner in the Secondary School	ed. M. F. Cleugh	Methuen
The Quality of Learning	R. Morris	Methuen
Music in Special Schools		The S.M.A.

(ii) Music Books for Teachers

Music through the Percussion Band	Y. Adair	Boosey & Hawkes
Music for the Handicapped Child	J. Alvin	OUP
Making Musical Apparatus and Instruments for use in Nursery and Infant Schools	K. Blocksidge	Nursery School Association
How to Use Melodic Percussion Instruments	K. Blocksidge	Nursery School Association
Music in Schools	J. Brocklehurst	Routledge
My Recorder Tune Book	F. Dinn	Schott
Making and Playing Bamboo Pipes	M. Galloway	Dryad Press
Play the Guitar	J. Gavall	Mills Music Ltd
The New Recorder Tutor	S. Goodyear	Mills Music Ltd
Music, Movement, and Mime for Children	V. Gray and R. Percival	OUP
The Pipers' Guild Handbook	M. James	Cramer
Percussion Playing	S. Moore	Paxton
Musical Instruments made to be Played	R. Roberts	Dryad Press
Infant Book (Oxford School Music Books)	W. Firth and J. P. B. Dobbs	OUP

APPENDIX B

SONGS AND SONG BOOKS

Section (i) lists songs with features which make them particularly suitable for the younger slow learners, and the sources from which they have been selected. Other books containing similar songs are given in Section (ii). Section (iii) lists songs which are more suitable for seniors—but it is likely that many of the songs from Sections (i) and (ii) will be equally popular with the older children. Section (iv) suggests some additional sources of senior songs.

(i)

Sources

A	Music Time	M. Wilson	OUP
B	A Third Sixty Songs for Little Children	H. Wiseman and S. Northcote	OUP
C	Children's Songs from Denmark	D. MacMahon	OUP
D	A European Folk-Song Book	J. Horton	E. J. Arnold
E	New Way Song Book	D. MacMahon	Schofield & Sims
F	English Songs for Children	P. Stack	Novello
G	Folk Songs of France	G. Reynolds	Boosey & Hawkes
H	Songs of the New World	D. MacMahon	McDougall
I	Twelve Songs of the Appalachian Mountains Bk. II	arr. I. Holst	OUP
J	Twenty-Five American Folk Songs for Young Singers		Schirmer (Chappell)

SONGS OF LIMITED RANGE

(a) *Compass of a fifth*

A	The old grey goose	D	Grass so green
	Summer, goodbye		Lullaby
B	The nightingale		Maytime
	The merry month of May		The cuckoo
C	Peter Hungry		The neighbours
	Clapper cake	G	Come and see my show
	Ride to the miller's house	H	Aunt Rhodie
	Sawing timber	I	The mocking bird
	Up, little John!		

(b) *Compass of a sixth*

A Susy, little Susy
Risha, rasha, rusha
Brown bread
My father's garden
The rascal

B The little swallow
Swinging
Scots hunting song
Tell me, shepherdess
A song for Easter Day

D Water Wagtail
Hey Betty Martin
Skip to my Lou

E The animals' dance
Away with melancholy
Daughter dear
The miller's wife

G By the shine of moonlight
Our donkey
When three chicks
Days of Christmas
Shoes and gloves
Sindy
The needle's eye
Dog and cat

Cumulative songs

D The little hill
E Fine is the little hen
If I were a boy

H Barnyard Song
I The farmyard

Songs with melodic repetition

A Susy, little Susy
Horses

B Come along
The nightingale
Anna Marie
Come home now
Bobby and Jean

C Peter Hungry
Abel Spendable
High on a tree
Tin soldiers

D Water wagtail
Grass so green

E Daughter dear
Mr. Baraban

F Oranges and lemons
Betty Anne

G By the shine of moonlight
The puss he went out walking
I'm a chubby little boy
We've at home five kittens

H Skip to my Lou
Springfield mountain

I The mocking bird

J The jolly miller
Nancy
Heirlooms
Chic-a-boom

Songs with word repetition

A Horses
My father's garden

B A farmyard song
Spin, spin

C Clapper cake
Tin soldiers
Up, little John!

F Soldier, soldier

H The little red wagon
The paw paw patch

J Til-a-mi-crac-in

Songs with mainly step-wise melodies

A	Brown bread	D	That's seven
	Will you come a-walking?	E	Fine is the little hen
	All my little ducks	F	The miller's wife
	Snowball	G	I'm a little chubby boy
B	Cuckoo	J	Plantation song
	God who made the earth		Heirlooms
	Jesus, friend of little		
	children		

Songs adaptable for two-chord accompaniment

A	The little boats	D	Green and white
	King and queen		Cuckoo
	The millwheel		Fine is the little hen
	The workmen		Daughter dear
	Jackie the sailor		Little Barbara
B	The little swallow	F	Merry ma-tansa
	My little donkey		London Bridge
	The maypole		Oranges and lemons
	Softly, softly	G	The cuckoo song
	Come home now		Come and see my show
C	Parade of the ducks		Brother Bernard
	Peter Hungry		Our donkey
	Clapper cake		There's no better stuff
	High on a tree	J	Plantation song
	Up, little John!		Shoes and gloves
D	Water wagtail		The jolly miller
	I would wed a tailor bold		Chic-a-boom
	Maytime		

Songs adaptable for three-chord accompaniment

A	It's raining	F	If I could have a windmill
	Will you come a-walking?		The old man from Hull
	My Aunt Jemima		The cow
	Guessing song		Rosy Apple
	Annabel's pussycat		Down by the riverside
B	Phoebe in her petticoat	G	A shepherdess one morning
	Money		Eat thy bread Marie
	Mr. Minitt		Come and see my show
	Dance with me		When three chicks
	Ducks, dogs and humans	H	Hey Betty Martin
C	Shoe my horse!		Mister Frog's wedding
	Sawing timber		Soldier, soldier
D	Green and white		

(ii)

Playtime Tunes (Bks. I & II)	M. Anderson	Cramer
Echo & Refrain Songs	E. Barnard	Stainer
New Nursery Jingles	E. Barnard	Curwen
Nursery School Musical Activities	E. Barnard	Curwen
Playing with sound	E. Barnard & M. G. Davies	Curwen
The Oxford Nursery Song Book	P. Buck	OUP
Song-Time	P. Dearmer & M. Shaw	Curwen
A Pre-School Music Book	A. Diller	Schirmer (Chappell)
Thirty Folk Settings for Children	A. Mendoza & J. Rimmer	Curwen
Seven Simple Songs for Children	A. Mendoza & J. Rimmer	Curwen
American Folk Songs for Children	R. Seeger	Doubleday
Seventeen Nursery Songs from the Appalachian Mountains	C. Sharp	Novello
Sixty Songs for Little Children	W. G. Whittaker, H. Wiseman, & J. Wishart	OUP
Second Sixty Songs for Little Children	W. G. Whittaker, H. Wiseman, & J. Wishart	OUP
Oxford School Music Books (Beginners) and (Juniors)		OUP
Eight Singing Games	W. I. Chitty	Paxton
Eight More Singing Games	W. I. Chitty	Paxton
Children's Traditional Singing Games Bks. I–V	Gomme & Sharp	Novello
Singing Games for Recreation Bks. I–V	J. Tobitt	Black
The Clarendon Books of Singing Games Bks. I & II	H. Wiseman & S. Northcote	OUP

(iii)

Sources

A	The Sundowners' Song Book	D. MacMahon	OUP
B	The Singing Cowboy	A. Veal	Boosey & Hawkes
C	Something to Sing, Vol. I	G. Brace	CUP
D	More Songs of the New World	D. MacMahon	McDougall
E	19 European Folk Songs	I. Holst	Novello
F	Folk Song and Guitar	J. Gavall	Curwen

A Lime juice tub
     The overlander
     The shearer's song
     The teams
     The dying stockman
     Goondiwindi
     Oh! the springtime
     The stockman's last bed
B The cowboy
     Big rock candy mountain
     The cowboy's lament
     Great grandad
     Home on the range
     Goodbye old paint
C The Gypsy Davey
     The Titanic
     Casey Jones
     On a British submarine
     The Fox
     Nellie Gray

D Boil them cabbage
     Buffalo girls
     Coming round the mountain
     Liza Jane
     Rye Whiskey
     Sweet Betsy
E Hark to the cuckoo
     O I did climb
     Spin, spin
     The white chestnut tree
     The cricket takes a wife
F The fisherman's evening song
     German peasant dance
     Flower girl
     Marianina
     Santa Lucia
     The life that's free
     The maypole
     The jolly farmer
     Lorelei
     Basque Lullaby

(iv)

Five Canadian Folk-Songs	Armstrong Gibbs	OUP
Burl Ives Song Book		Ballantine Books
Burl Ives Sea Songs		Ballantine Books
Something to Sing, Vol. II	G. Brace	CUP
Twelve Sea Shanties	J. Clements	OUP
The American Song Book	J. Horton	E. J. Arnold
Twelve Songs from Jamaica	Murray & Gavall	OUP
Sing a Round	M. Wilson	OUP
Firsts and Seconds	Appleby & Fowler	OUP

APPENDIX C

(i) *Records which introduce a variety of sounds and noises*

Each title represents an EP record.

Car effects; Church bells; Dogs; Horses (galloping, trotting); Sea effects (wash on shingle and seagulls); Ships' sirens and hooters; Thunderstorms; Trains; Wind; Birds (dawn chorus, nightingale and owls); Street noises; Aeroplanes; Space-ships, and ghosts; Telephone bell; Footsteps and marching; Farmyard effects; Jungle noises; Electronic sound patterns.

(ii) *Records from which songs can be learnt*

Nursery Rhymes	Doris Gould
Old Dutch Rhymes	John Langstaff
English & American Folk Songs	John Langstaff
Singing Games	John Langstaff
Noah's Ark & Other Songs	William Clauson
A Froggie would a-wooing go and Other Songs	William Clauson
Listen Now	William Clauson
Let's Pretend	Gladys Whitred & Richard Dawson
Folk Song Today	ed. P. Kennedy
John Langstaff Sings	
Shanties from the Seven Seas	Stan Hugill
The Midnight Thief	R. R. Bennett

(iii) *Records introducing various instruments*

Hit the Note Series   1. Grand Piano
                           2. The Voice in the Secret Box (violin)
                           3. Baby Piano (celesta)

Once upon a Time   The Bremen Street Musicians
                   The Shepherdess and the Sweep
                   The Sweet Shop on Beat Street   } K. Rattenbury
                   The Tinder Box

Listen Now   Listen Now
                The Town Musicians   W. Clauson

Tunes for Children   arr. R. Fiske

Instruments of the Orchestra   introduced by Yehudi Menuhin

Teachers are advised to consult the catalogue issued by The Education Department of E.M.I. Records Ltd (20 Manchester Square, London, W.1) for the current numbers of these records.

(iv) *Records for General Listening*

Records marked with an asterisk are more suitable for older pupils.

Bach/Walton	Sheep may safely graze
Benjamin	Jamaican Rumba*
Borodin	Polovtsian Dances*
Clarke	Trumpet Voluntary
Delibes	Mazurka from *Coppélia*
De Severac	Musical Box
Dukas	L'Apprenti Sorcier
Elgar	Pomp and Circumstance March No. 1
Grainger	Mock Morris
Granados	Spanish Dance in E Min.
Grieg	In the Hall of the Mountain King and Anitra's Dance from *Peer Gynt*
Handel	Minuet from *Berenice*
Haydn	Trumpet Concerto
Holst	Jupiter and Mars from *The Planets**
Mendelssohn	Nocturne and Wedding March from *A Midsummer Night's Dream*
	Fingal's Cave Overture*
Mozart	Eine Kleine Nachtmusik
Nielsen	Dance of the Cockerels from *Maskarade*
Ravel	Bolero
	Mother Goose Suite
Rimsky Korsakov	The Flight of the Bumble Bee*
Rossini	William Tell Overture*
Saint-Saëns	Elephant, Birds, Fossils, The Swan from *The Carnival of the Animals*
Schubert	Ballet Music from *Rosamunde*
	Marche Militaire
Smetana	Polka from *The Bartered Bride*
	The Moldau
Stravinsky	The *Fire Bird* Suite*
Tchaikovsky	The *Nutcracker* Suite
Vaughan Williams	Greensleeves Fantasia
	March: Folk Songs from Somerset from *English Folk-Song Suite*
Walton	Popular Song from *Façade*
Weinberger	Polka from *Schwanda the Bagpiper*

Famous Tunes from the Classics—33 SX13941

APPENDIX D

FILM STRIPS

The Strings, Woodwind, Brass, Percussion	Unicorn Head Visual Aids Ltd 42 Westminster Palace Gardens, Artillery Row, London S.W.1
Instruments of the Orchestra	Ministry of Education Curzon Street, London W.1
The Sorcerer's Apprentice	Education Productions Ltd
Peter and the Wolf	East Ardsley, Wakefield, Yorks

APPENDIX E

Books and music for use in connection with Chapter 6—Movement and Dance.

Modern Educational Dance	Laban (revised Ullmann)	Macdonald and Evans
Handbook for Modern Educational Dance	Preston	Macdonald and Evans
Modern Dance in Education	Russell	Macdonald and Evans
Drama in Education	Alington	Basil Blackwell
Dance and Dance Drama in Education	Bruce	Pergamon Press

Piano Music

For children (Vols I and II)	Bartók	Boosey & Hawkes
Children's Pieces	Kabalevsky	Boosey & Hawkes
Album for the Young	Schumann	Augener
Scenes from Childhood	Schumann	Augener

Gramophone records

The items marked with an asterisk are useful for work of a dramatic nature.

Bax	Tintagel*
Berlioz	Symphonie Fantastique*
Clarke	Trumpet Voluntary
Debussy	Children's Corner Suite
Delibes	Coppélia Ballet Suite
Dukas	L'Apprenti Sorcier*
Fauré	Dolly Suite
Grieg	Peer Gynt Suite No. 1

Gramophone records

Holst	Mars from *The Planets**
Mendelssohn	The Hebrides Overture*
Prokofiev	March from *Love for Three Oranges*
Quilter	Children's Overture
Saint-Saëns	The Carnival of the Animals
	Danse Macabre*
Warlock	Capriol Suite

APPENDIX F

USEFUL ADDRESSES

The Association for Special Education	c/o National Secretary, Hallmoor Sec. Special School, Lea Hall, Birmingham 33
Journal: *Special Education* (Quarterly)	12 Park Crescent, London, W.1
The Guild of Teachers of Backward Children Journal: *Forward Trends* (Quarterly)	7 Albemarle Street, London W.1
The National Society for Mentally Handicapped Children Journal: *Parents' Voice* (Quarterly)	5 Bulstrode Street, London W.1
The National Association of the Teachers of the Mentally Handicapped Journal: *Teaching and Training* (Quarterly)	43 Queen Anne Street, London W.1
The National Association for Mental Health Journal: *Mental Health* (Bi-monthly)	39 Queen Ann Street, London W.1
The Society for Music Therapy and Remedial Music	48 Lanchester Road, London N.6

Publications: Members' bulletin and Conference papers

APPENDIX G

MUSIC PUBLISHERS

E. J. Arnold & Co Ltd	Butterley Street, Leeds 10
Ed. Arnold Ltd (Novellos)	Borough Green, Sevenoaks, Kent
Augener Ltd (Galliard)	148 Charing Cross Road, London, W.C.2
Ballantine Books	101 5th Avenue New York, U.S.A.

(Agent: Transworld Publishers Ltd, Park Royal, London, N.W.10)

A. & C. Black Ltd	4 Soho Square, London, W.1
Boosey & Hawkes	295 Regent Street, London, W.1
Cambridge University Press (CUP)	Bentley House, 200 Euston Road, London, N.W.1
Chappell & Co. Ltd	50 New Bond Street, London, W.1
J. B. Cramer & Co. Ltd	139 New Bond Street, London, W.1
J. Curwen & Sons Ltd	29 Maiden Lane, London, W.C.2
Doubleday	Garden City, New York, U.S.A.
Elkin & Co. Ltd (Novello)	Borough Green, Sevenoaks, Kent
M. Hohner Ltd	11–13 Farringdon Road, London, E.C.1
Alfred A. Kalmus	2/3 Fareham Street, Dean Street, London, W.1
McDougall's Educational Co.	30 Royal Terrace, Edinburgh
Mills Music Ltd	20 Denmark Street, London, W.C.2
Novello & Co. Ltd	Borough Green, Sevenoaks, Kent
Oxford University Press (OUP)	44 Conduit Street, London, W.1
W. Paxton & Co. Ltd	36–38 Dean Street, London, W.1
Schofield and Sims	35 St John's Road, Huddersfield, Yorks
Schott & Co Ltd	48 Gt. Marlborough Street, London, W.1
Stainer & Bell Ltd	Lesbourne Road, Reigate, Surrey

Index